Re-Imagining God: A Spiritual Journey

*A former Presbyterian minister offers his most personal of stories in the hope that
it might suggest to readers some fresh ways of imagining their
own personal responses to the mystery that lies at the heart of our existence.*

Re-Imagining
GOD

A Spiritual Journey

Lucius DuBose

COLD RIVER STUDIO
NASHVILLE, TENNESSEE

Cold River Studio is an independent press committed to introducing fresh, exciting voices to the reading public. It is our mission to take a chance on deserving authors and achieve the highest quality when bringing their words to the marketplace. We believe in the power of words and ideas and strive to introduce readers to new, creative writers.

Published by Cold River Studio, Nashville, Tennessee

First Edition: March 2010

Printed in the United States of America
ISBN 978-0-9842298-6-4

FOR LENDA,
without whom none of this

Contents

Re-Imagining God: A Spiritual Journey

. . . it is the mind
Turned away from the world
That turns against it.

—Wendell Berry
Window Poems #13

INTRODUCTION

"HAVE YOU LOST your faith?"

My father's question caught me completely by surprise; although, it probably shouldn't have. After all, it didn't exactly come right out of the blue. Indeed, it was the product of a long and difficult history of father-son relations. It was Christmas and I was visiting in my parents' home for the first time after several years of alienation and angry silence. Six years earlier, after spending ten years as a Presbyterian minister, a role in which I had found little satisfaction, I had finally given up my ordination for a career as an artist and a member of a college art faculty. My father was so disturbed by that decision that he had hardly spoken to me since. While it wasn't the only reason for his anger, my decision to leave the ministry seemed to be the straw that broke an already strained relationship. The ministry had always been my family's dream for me, and he took my quitting it as a betrayal of the promise he and my mother had seen in me and as a personal slap in the face after all he had invested in my upbringing and education.

Now, sadly, he was an old man. The years and failing health had worn down his anger, so I took his question to be part of an awkward attempt at reconciliation. I think he was genuinely baffled and troubled by the path my life had taken, and he was sincerely trying to understand. But he just couldn't seem to get past his long-held preconceptions about who I was. I had never been able to share with him anything about the struggles I had been through, the emotional and intellectual anguish I had experienced trying to fit into a role for which I was so temperamentally ill equipped. He had no idea what it meant to be an artist or a teacher of art, having had almost no formal education beyond the eighth grade. But he had been so absolutely certain that he knew better than I did what was right for me that he could only conceive of my sudden change in direction as the result of some kind of spiritual breakdown.

To one who had known me for as long as he had, my sudden departure from the ministry must indeed have seemed a breathtakingly abrupt reversal in direction and a disturbingly radical change in lifestyle. From the day— having hardly gotten home from the maternity ward—I was added to the "Cradle Roll" of the Arsenal Hill Presbyterian Church in Columbia, South Carolina, I had seemed almost "predestined" for the religious vocation. It was as if I had been born into a force field that was drawing me in that direction as surely as a magnetic compass points irresistibly north. I think I must have known from early childhood that when I grew up, the pulpit was where I would find myself on all the Sundays of my life. And that is where I had been, though not as comfortably as I had expected, for the last ten years of Sundays. Then, on February 1, 1969, I simply stepped down, as it were, out of the pulpit of the Westminster Presbyterian Church in Nashville, dropped my velvet-paneled black robe on the floor of the chancel, stripped off my clerical collar, marched resolutely down the center aisle, out of the great sanctuary doors, and closed them firmly behind me. And I had never been back. Once I entered the thoroughly secular world of the art studio and the college classroom, the only times I ever found myself even sitting in a church pew again were for weddings or funerals. I had said good-bye forever to my religious home place. Or so I thought.

It wasn't until my wife, Lenda, and I were married, almost eight years to the day after I had walked out of the Church, that I began to look back and sort through the baggage left over from my religious past. Ironically, she had grown up in Westminster Church herself and, in fact, had been married there before moving away from Nashville only a few months before I arrived in the mid sixties. Now divorced, she had returned to Nashville with her two daughters and was employed in the student center at Vanderbilt University. By then, I was an Assistant Professor on the art faculty at Peabody College just across the street. On the night of Jimmy Carter's presidential election, I was hosting an election night party in my apartment for a group of art department colleagues and students. A former graduate student of ours who lived in my same apartment complex, and who was also working in the Vanderbilt student center, had asked me if she could invite a friend to my party. She said she thought this friend was someone I might enjoy meeting. The party was in full swing when there was a knock at my door. "Hi, I'm Lenda," she announced with as beautiful a smile as I had ever seen. As soon as the door closed behind her we started to talk, and we haven't stopped talking since. Our marriage, exactly three months later, was just a pause in the conversation that has been going on now for over thirty years.

Like me, Lenda was born into the Presbyterian church. Unlike me, however, her early indoctrination into the faith did not really take. As early as the fifth grade, she began to ask questions in Sunday school about things she was being taught that didn't make any sense to her. And no one, it seemed, had ever been able to answer those questions to her satisfaction. Now she began to put them to me. We didn't just talk about religion, though. We talked about art, music, poetry, books, politics, nature, science, history, people, relationships, children, death, you name it. Still, religion has been a recurring theme of many long discussions. But theological questions were, for her, not simply a matter of intellectual game playing. Her questions were serious and personal, and she was no more willing to accept glib answers from me than she was from her fifth grade Sunday school teacher. Among her many intellectual interests is a questing curiosity about geology and astronomy, and she was not about to consent to any kind of "God talk" that did not harmonize with her sense of geological time and of the astronomical immensity of the universe. As a very young child she had developed a deep-seated fear of abandonment as a result of her mother's emotional detachment, and her resulting hunger for connectedness, in both a human and a cosmic sense, lent an existential urgency to our discussions of spirituality and religion, church teaching and personal belief, and the meanings of our lives and of our deaths. It was out of those searching conversations—mostly during countless hours at the mealtime table—that the impetus was born in me to undertake a thorough reexamination of the faith that had so completely dominated the first half of my life, to bring up to date—for better or worse—whatever of my early religious convictions I still retained, and to attempt to put to rest once and for all my father's anguished question.

"Have you lost your faith?" His question had caught me off guard because, though the Church had been central to the life of our family for as long as I could remember, he and I had never had a serious discussion about our personal beliefs. For that matter I don't recall many discussions at all on any subject. What we had had all of my life were mostly arguments (or one-sided moralizing "sermons" from him), and I was weary of contending with him. So what could I say to his question? How could I give him some assurance about my "spiritual condition" and still be honest with myself? I don't recall exactly what I said. It was something to the effect that what I had always believed had not really changed; it was just that I was no longer comfortable with traditional religious language. Of course, he had no idea what I was talking about, but he didn't pursue the matter any further, and, regretfully, we never got any closer to a real meeting of the minds before he died.

In the first chapter of what I have called the "re-imagining" of the faith of my youth, I have attempted—though it sadly comes three decades too late for him—to make up for that lost opportunity to help my father to understand my discomfort with the language of belief. My response to him back then was an accurate, if hopelessly incomplete, statement of one of the critical issues in my decision to give up my religious calling: the failure of traditional religious language to serve as an adequate medium for thinking and talking about spiritual/religious questions in today's new world. I believe that for many people today the "words" of their inherited faith are losing, or have already lost, their meaning and thus have become stumbling blocks in the quest for a deeper, more meaningful spirituality. And there is a simple reason for that failure and our need for new "coins of exchange" if our spiritual/religious dialogue is to achieve a new vitality. The following four chapters examine four other "stumbling block" issues: organized religion (the difference between spirituality and religion and what happens when spirituality is institutionalized); authority in religion (the Bible and the fundamentalist error); science and religion (more specifically, evolution and its importance for an understanding of human spirituality); and the problem of evil (traditional Christianity's failure to address adequately the causes of human-self-destructive and community-destructive behavior). Chapter six is perhaps the pivotal chapter. In it I propose a turning away from the "supernaturalism" of Western religious belief toward a whole new down-to-earth story as a way of giving new form to our spiritual response to the mysteries that surrounds our daily existence. In the final two chapters, I have tried first to suggest a new way of thinking about prayer as a means to "connectedness," and finally I have chanced a tentative glimpse at the nagging business of what happens to us when we die. Throughout the book, as a sort of subtext to the main theme, there emerges repeatedly a concern for the way in which our notions about the deity and our relationship to "Him" have affected our relationship to the natural world and to the other creatures that share our home place. Our "adversarial" stance with regard to our environment, which has brought into peril our very future as a species and the future of our planet as a life-supporting habitat, stems at least in part, I believe, from our typical Western way of envisioning and worshipping a God who exists as a separate being apart from his creation. And that needs to change.

At the beginning of this endeavor, I received some very good advice from my oldest friend. I had sent him the first drafts of some early chapters for his advice and critique. His response was encouraging, but he felt that the tone of the writing was wrong somehow; it was too academic, too much like a thesis addressed to scholarly intellectuals to appeal to the ordinary person to whom I should be writing. I needed to get of off my "high horse" and remember who my real audience was. Finally, he said to me, "Loosh, just tell your own story."

And that is what I have tried to do. On the one hand, this is a story of what was lost, the erosion of a youthful faith, the death of an honest dream, the failure of a guiding vision. But it is also the story of the recovery of sight and insight, the defining of new and different expectations, and the reconstruction of a belief more adequate for the new world in which I find myself today. During the time that I was putting all this into words, there has been a constant and changing assortment of real people who, in my imagination, sat opposite me at my desk, to whom I was trying my best to make sense of my thoughts on spirituality and religion. I apologize to them if my efforts to reach out to them where they live have fallen short. I need, however, in all honesty, to confess that it was not primarily for them that I undertook to put all this together in the first place. In writing this I was doing what every artist is always doing, no matter what his medium: giving form to his peculiar vision of what it is to be human in the world. This is my attempt to bring some sense and order to the disparate ways in which I personally have responded to life, to gather together the disjointed segments of my journey into one continuous path. And even if no one else should ever read this story, the time and labor that went into it was worth the effort. But hardly any artist of whatever stripe will deny that when the work of putting a very private and personal vision into form is complete, there always comes the desire to share that work with others. So, I offer this most personal of stories to the public, in the hope that it might suggest, to any who should take the time to read it, some fresh ways of imagining his or her own personal responses to the mystery that lies at the heart of our existence.

WORDS, WORDS, WORDS

*Speaking the unspeakable, describing the
indescribable, defining the indefinable*

MY FUMBLING ANSWER to my father's question all those
years ago obviously did not satisfy his concern for the state
of my spiritual welfare. But he didn't persist. He let it drop
without insisting that I clarify what I was trying to say.
And what if he hadn't just let it go? What if he had said
something like, "What do you mean, you're not comfortable
with traditional religious language? What are you talking
about?" What would I have said then? How could I have
explained to him, in terms that he could understand, the
difficulty I was having with the "words" of the religious faith
in which I had been nurtured?

He was not an educated man, though neither was he
unintelligent. Born in 1900 in rural South Carolina, he
dropped out of school after the eighth grade and left home
at the early age of sixteen to seek a life away from the farm
where he was raised. After working a number of different
jobs into his early twenties, he realized that he needed more
training if he was to get anywhere in the world—especially
now that he had met and fallen in love with the young woman
who was to be my mother—so he enrolled in a business
school where he took courses in accounting. He apparently

excelled in numbers, for, upon completion of the course, he immediately landed a job with a large insurance company where he worked until retirement. And he did well. In 1942 he was chosen to head up the company's district office in Birmingham, Alabama, where we moved when I was ten (he was the only one of eight siblings ever to have moved farther than forty miles from where he was born). He was a hard worker, a devoted husband, but an unaffectionate and authoritarian father. He was not a particularly spiritual person; the Presbyterian Church and its activities seemed to be his only religion. If he ever read the Bible or engaged in prayer other that his mumbled mealtime blessings, I was never aware of it. I don't believe he ever read a book in his life. Perusing the daily paper was about the sum of his intellectual activity.

So, how was I going to explain to this man what I was talking about when I said that I was having trouble with the language of traditional religion? Had he pursued the issue back then, I am not sure I could have said much more than I did at the time because I hadn't really thought through the problem myself. But that issue—how we talk and think about spiritual things, the nature of religious language—was an important factor in my decision to leave the ministry, and I missed a chance to attempt to explain what was troubling me, and perhaps to help him understand more about where I was. What follows in this chapter is, in a way, an effort to make up for that missed opportunity, a kind of overdue letter to my father.

Dad, let me see if I can explain what I meant when I said that I was having trouble with traditional religious language. We're talking about words now and how we use them to talk about things that are hard to describe, okay? Now, I remember, from when I was a boy, some words I used to hear you say whenever you wanted to describe a really attractive young woman. I know this was not entirely original to you, but I don't think I ever heard anyone else use this particular figure of speech. Do you remember what I'm talking about? You used to say, "She's as pretty as a..."

(And I can hear him now completing the sentence, "...as pretty as a speckled puppy," no doubt with a smile of recollection.)

"...as pretty as a speckled puppy." And you know why that saying seemed perfectly natural coming from you, don't you?

(He would know, of course. When I was a child, my father, having learned to love animals while growing up on the farm, became a breeder of thoroughbred, registered cocker spaniel dogs. We owned a female named Lady of Columbia, who was a deep chocolate brown. Every time a new litter of puppies arrived [I never knew exactly how they got there; my father's generation didn't believe in sex education] most of them always seemed to be colored solidly like their mother, either brown or black. But there was almost always one who was a mixture of white and black or brown, and that beautiful "speckled puppy" was the pick of the litter.)

You and I know that your special way of expressing your admiration for a pretty girl was to compare her with the singular beauty of a little multicolored cocker spaniel. But what if you had said that in the presence of someone who had never seen a litter of newborn puppies, who perhaps didn't even know that they came in a variety of color patterns, or who was a cat lover and had no admiration at all for the beauty of dogs? Can you see how such a person might not appreciate what you were saying, just might not get it? And a lot of people nowadays might even feel that you were being chauvinistic and insulting, comparing a young woman to a puppy. We know that you didn't mean it that way, but you see, don't you, how words whose meaning we take for granted can often be misunderstood and sometime not be taken as we mean them to be.

Now, suppose you got to know that pretty young woman a little better and discovered that her personality didn't match her outward beauty and you wanted some way to convey what she was really like. She is troublesome and complaining and hard to get along with. How would you describe the inner qualities of this person who, on the outside, might be "as pretty as a speckled puppy," but not on the inside? There are a lot of words you might choose, depending on her personality type, but let me suggest one from a famous piece of literature. William Shakespeare wrote a play about such a woman, the comedy drama titled *The Taming of the Shrew*.[1] It is the story of a husband's attempt to control the behavior of his wife who is beautiful, but rebellious, hot tempered, and quarrelsome. It made for a wonderfully funny play. The term "shrew" was commonly used to describe such an ill-humored, contrary wife, so the people of Shakespeare's day understood perfectly what the play was about even before they saw it. However, "shrew" is not a term that one would likely be heard using today. Most modern people have never seen a shrew, or even know what one is—a tiny, not very pleasant mouse-like animal with a pointed nose and narrow-set eyes, who is very aggressive in going after the insects that it devours voraciously. So, because that word is not part of our common vocabulary today, it wouldn't resonate with us as it once might have. There are some other words (which I won't mention here) that we might be more likely to use today. Remember also that in Shakespeare's day, a wife was expected to be obedient and submissive to her husband, and so a spouse who tended to challenge her husband's authority was seen in a very different light than she would be today. In the sixteenth century she might commonly be thought of as a shrew, whereas in the twenty-first century she might just as likely be admired as an independent and strongly self-possessed woman.

Now, I know you're wondering just what all this has to do with my questions about religious language. But stick with me a bit longer; I think you'll see where this is going. Here's the question I'm trying to get at: how do you talk about—or even think about—something that you cannot see? It can't be seen, heard, smelled, tasted, or touched. It can't be weighed or measured. And yet, somehow, we hang on to the idea that it is real. I'm talking here, of course, about God, about spiritual reality. And that's the problem with the whole business of religious belief and with religious language in particular: how do you talk or think about something that lies outside of your ordinary frame of reference? This is not a chair or an automobile or your next-door neighbor we're talking about. This is something you say you believe in, but which you cannot approach with your usual senses or describe directly.

You'll probably be saying at this point, "Well, I guess you just have to take it on faith." Yes, but faith in what? How do you begin to *say* what you believe? And that was what I was getting paid to do as a minister. Remember the old joke about the young minister who was nervous about his first sermon? He went to an older minister and asked him what he should preach about, and the older man told him, "Preach about God, and preach about twenty minutes." Well, that's what I was supposed to do every Sunday, get up in the pulpit and *say* something about God. And how was I to do that? Well, I could only do exactly what you did when you compared the hard-to-describe beauty of a pretty girl to the beauty of a speckled puppy; I had to use figures of speech. I had to use what English teachers call metaphors. The dictionary defines a metaphor as "a figure of speech in which a term or a phrase is applied to something to which it is not literally applicable in order to suggest a resemblance, as in *A mighty fortress is our God.*"[2]. That's what Shakespeare was doing when he called that troublesome wife a shrew. He didn't mean that she was literally a beady-eyed, voracious little animal, but using that word for her was his way of making more real to the reader what her personality was like (if the reader— or playgoer—knew anything at all about shrews). You weren't saying that that lovely young woman looked like a puppy; you were applying a term that was not literally applicable to her as a way of making her beauty more tangible (if your listener knew anything at all about how pretty little multicolored cocker spaniels are). And what I am trying to help you to see is that such figures of speech are the only way we have of saying what we believe, of talking about the deity and the things of the spirit. There is no other way of talking about the object of religious belief except by use of metaphors. And there are positives and negatives about that.

There is a favorite poem of mine that illustrates the power of this kind of figure of speech. It's by the American poet Carl Sandburg, and it's titled simply "Fog":

> *The fog comes*
> *on little cat feet.*
>
> *It sits looking*
> *over harbor and city*
> *on silent haunches*
> *and then moves on.*[3]

In those few lines, by using the cat and its distinctive way of moving and being still as a figure of speech, a metaphor, for the fog, the poet has told us more about how the fog acts on our awareness than any kind of weatherman's description of atmospheric causes and effects could ever do. Just as Shakespeare did with the use of the shrew as a figure of speech, Sandburg has used the image of the cat to capture and convey a certain intangible quality that the fog has that can only be described in this indirect way. The strict literalist might protest that fog doesn't have feet; it doesn't walk and it doesn't have haunches to sit on, nor eyes for looking. Yet there is a truth here that cannot be revealed to us by the literal scientific facts. If we are open to the poetic use of that kind of figure of speech, we will learn a truth that cannot be communicated in any other way, and chances are, after reading this short poem, we may never experience fog in quite the same way again. The metaphor makes available to us qualities—reveals to us truths, if you will—that we have no other way of grasping. And that is exactly how religious language works.

For some time now I have had the notion that the best way to make theological education more effective for those who are training to be ministers, priests, rabbis, teachers, and interpreters of religious tradition would be to require two years of intensive study of poetry—all kinds of poetry—and nothing else, before they are allowed to begin biblical and theological studies. That's facetious, of course; it will never happen. But if it did, I am convinced that we would be spared a lot of the nonsense that biblical literalists and religious fundamentalists are always trying to foist off on us. I began to form that idea after I first read the Genesis epic of creation in the original Hebrew and felt the impact of its dramatic poetry. I was not a Hebrew scholar, but I did study it enough to get a feel for the language. The first chapter of Genesis has nothing to do with *how* the world came into being, or how *long* it took; it is a poetic celebration of the meaning of its existence. The problem that plagues the literally minded and fundamentalists of all shapes is that they just don't seem to understand the difference between *truth* and *fact*. The two are not necessarily the same.

Is it a *fact* that "fog comes on little cat feet"? No, of course not. No more than it is a fact that pretty girls look like speckled puppies. But is it the truth? Is it true that there is a universal quality to beauty that can be shared by two creatures that are otherwise completely different? And is it true that fog has about it the quality described by the poet's metaphor? It is true if you have the imagination to see the connection (that's what reading poetry helps you to get). Is it a *fact* that the heavens and the earth were created in seven days? No, of course not; science has taught us that the world could not have begun like that. Is, therefore, the great hymn of origins in Genesis, ascribing purpose and meaning to the existence of the earth and its inhabitants, *untrue*? I suppose that depends upon your religious belief, your spiritual imagination—or lack thereof—but whether it is true or not does not depend upon some literal interpretation of such phrases as, "In the beginning God created the heavens and the earth…" or "And God said, 'Let there be light'…" or " On the seventh day He rested…" etc., etc. Those are not facts in the same way that the statement, "Lucius DuBose graduated from college with a BA in English in June, 1954" is a fact. They belong to a different order of truth. They belong to the realm of poetic truth, a kind of truth that is truer than mere facts, that goes deeper than mere scientific

17

or historical reporting to get at the meaning of the facts. And the odd thing is that neither those who would defend the Genesis account of creation as literal history, nor those who reject it as fiction seem to understand that distinction.

You see, all religious language is metaphorical. All the words I used to use when preaching and teaching about the object of my faith were figures of speech, because I had no other way to talk about it. I had no other way to say what I believed. Remember the definition of metaphor that I cited earlier: "…a figure of speech in which a term or a phrase is applied to something to which it is not literally applicable in order to suggest a resemblance, as in *A mighty fortress is our God*." God is not literally a "mighty fortress," but for some who believe that their faith provides them a safe haven from the storms of life, He may be *like* a mighty fortress. He is not literally the "maker of all things" as a carpenter is literally the maker of the chair, leg by leg and rung by rung. He is somehow, to religious people, the source and meaning of all that exists, even the things for which they have no literally descriptive words. To say that another way, when, over the centuries, people have sensed that there is a mystery about life in the universe that transcends the mundane commonality of their existence, they have applied the name "God" to that mystery. Even that word is a metaphor for a reality that we cannot describe literally. He is not literally "our father," as you are literally my parent; He is like a father to those who believe in a loving and compassionate deity who personally watches over His creation. He is not even literally a "he." Spiritual reality has no gender. So, none of the words we use to express our faith can be taken literally. How could they be? God (whatever we mean by the word) is not approachable directly, nor definable in human terms. Whenever people have attempted to talk or think about the meaning of the mystery they sense around them, whenever they have tried to say what they believe about that mystery, they have been forced to fall back on terms that were familiar to them from their experiences of daily life—*creator, lord, king, father, savior, master, mighty fortress*—and apply them to the indefinable reality to make it more real and more approachable, just as the poet used the image of the cat to make more real the intangible qualities of the fog. The words are not the truth itself; they are the doorways to a level of truth that cannot be approached in any other way. This does not lessen the validity of the language. It doesn't take anything away from the value or truth of the Genesis account of creation to say that it cannot be taken literally. Quite the contrary, it is the biblical literalist who devalues the account by insisting on treating it as mere objective, historical fact, something that it was never intended to be. It is the fundamentalists with their desperate need to reduce every truth to verifiable, scientific fact who have demeaned the Bible, and thus played into the hands of the cynics who would deny the validity of any and all religious language. And in so doing, the very people who claim loudest to revere the Bible are the same ones who have robbed it of its power and its profundity.

I can think of no better illustration of the unique power of metaphorical language than the well-known Twenty-Third

Psalm from the Old Testament. We all know how it starts:

> *The Lord is my Shepherd; I shall not want.*
> *He maketh me to lie down in green pastures:*
> *He leadeth me beside the still waters.*
> *He restoreth my soul:*
> *He leadeth me in the path of righteousness*
>   *for His name's sake.*
> *Yea, though I walk through the valley of*
>   *the shadow of death,*
> *I will fear no evil: for Thou art with me;*
> *Thy rod and thy staff they comfort me…"*
>   (Psalm 23, KJV)

One of the most significant things about this great hymn of consolation and hope is almost lost in translation. The word for "Lord" in Hebrew is *Adonai*, which was used by the Jews of Old Testament times as a spoken substitute for the unutterable name of the deity, *Jahweh*. So holy, so remote from human intimacy, so unapproachable directly was their God, *Jahweh*, that they were forbidden even to speak His name. This was the "wholly other," terrible in His power, jealous in his demand for obedience, swift to punish. And the psalmist dared to say, "*Adonai* is my *Shepherd*." He did nothing less than take two terms almost completely opposite in impact and put them together to form a brand new metaphor for the deity, and in that one simple but brilliantly inspired leap of the imagination, he may well have changed the Judeo-Christian concept of God forever. By applying to this remote and forbidding deity the attributes of a compassionate shepherd, he creates a whole new image of God. Such is the revelatory power of an inspired figure of speech.

Before I leave the Twenty-Third Psalm, however, there is one other thing that I'd like you to think about. As powerful and as revolutionary as the image of the shepherd was when applied to the notion of a remote and distant deity, it is not a metaphor that is likely to resonate familiarly with many citizens of the twenty-first century. I'm afraid that the full power of that inspired insight is lost on this generation, because most of us have never even seen a shepherd, certainly not the kind the psalmist had in mind (the last shepherd I saw was riding a four-wheeled Honda ATV). That takes us right back to what I was trying to get at when I said that I had grown uncomfortable with traditional religious language.

In the latter days of my tenure in the ministry, I began to feel that the words with which I had grown so familiar over the years were going dead on me. Talking about belief was my job, and I was good at it. The one place I had always been most comfortable as a minister was in the pulpit. I was confident of my verbal skills; I believed in the power of the spoken word. My ambition had always been to follow in the footsteps of the great pulpiteers, to be a great preacher—in the best sense of that word—a communicator, an interpreter, an effective proclaimer of the "Good News" of the Christian Gospel, a teller of the "old story" who could make it relevant to a new generation. Yet, when I attempted to do that, the language I was accustomed to using, the religious and theological words of the "old story" which I had been brought up on and had seriously studied for so many years, seemed like a foreign tongue. It wasn't, as you put it, that I had "lost my faith." It was that when I tried to talk about, or even think about that faith, the old words like God, Christ, sin, salvation, resurrection, heaven, hell, and all the rest of those "creedal" words we were so accustomed to tossing about in the Church, just seemed to be lifeless and empty. And even more troubling, I had lost my confidence in the currency of the language as a valid coin of exchange between me and the person in the pew. I had no assurance that those familiar words of our "common faith" had a common meaning any longer. It felt as if I had been struck dumb. Without a common language, I no longer knew how to talk about what I believed, and that was very frustrating. For the first time in my religious experience, I was literally at a loss for words.

What was happening? The problem, I think, was precisely that all of our shepherds were driving ATVs! All of the language of faith—the metaphors, the figures of speech that had once enabled believers like me to make tangible the intangible spiritual realities—came from a world that no longer existed. After all, the standard words of faith that I was still using in the late twentieth century did not, for the most part, arise out of my own personal, individual search for ways of connecting with the mystery of my own existence; they were words that were just handed down *to* me from past generations, defined *for* me as truths that I should simply accept. I didn't come up with the standard words that I found myself using when I tried to talk about belief. When they originally came into use, they were probably the hard won products of real peoples' vital search for meaning, but those people lived centuries before I was born, in a world I never knew. The whole point of metaphorical language—the comparative figures of speech that enable us to communicate about those qualities that are hard to describe directly, whether it be a speckled puppy for the indescribable beauty of a pretty girl, a shrew for the quarrelsome personality of a contrary wife, a cat for the mysterious qualities of fog, or a shepherd for the compassionate nature of a distant deity— is that those comparative words are drawn from our real experience of the daily world in which we live. And all of the metaphors, the figures of speech that made up the language of belief, my native tongue, had come from worlds that no longer existed. Our world has undergone radical changes since the common religious figures of speech came into use. The medieval, pre-scientific, pre-psychological world in which those terms originated is long gone. Our whole feeling for the "geography" of the universe has been altered. Heaven is no longer *up* there and hell is no longer *down* there because our ventures into outer space have shown us that there is no up or down. There is no "place" in our modern imaginations for a "place" called heaven. The deity who was "King, Lord, and Master" has gone the way of earthly kings and lords and masters. Most of them have been overthrown. And the "Mighty Fortresses" are now mostly crumbling tourist attractions. Sin and guilt have been replaced in our vocabularies by psychological complexes, sociological maladjustment, and genetic disorders. Our familiarity with dysfunctional families makes it problematical to use "Our Father" as a symbol for ultimate truth and the source of all that is good. And "He," as a capitalized pronoun for deity, will not work in an age marked by the significant shifting of gender roles and the changing shape of marriage. There is no "Man Upstairs" because there is no upstairs and "He" is not a he.

Over the years I have come to realize that what I was feeling with regard to the common language of the faith was by no means peculiar to me. And the problem was not that those who belong to this spiritually disconnected age do not believe in an ultimate truth that transcends their merely physical existence. It isn't that we do not believe any longer that there is a way to be connected to the "Mystery." It is, rather, that the standard connectors are worn out and faulty. And I don't believe that it does much good to continue flipping the same old switches on and off in hope that lights will somehow come on again. That is one of the main reasons for my leaving the pulpit. I could not in all honesty go on repeating the same old formulas once they had lost their validity for me. I know that there are those who think that if we just say the old words loudly and often enough we will find our way back to the old certainties, that the answer to so-called modern relativism is to get "back to the Bible," or to put prayer back in the schools, or display the Ten Commandments in public places. But I can't believe that by going backward, by submitting ourselves to any traditional religious authority that we will find long-term answers to the anxieties we feel in response to the shifting boundaries of modern life. Nor would it seem to me that just giving the old forms a new look and a new sound is going to make a lot of difference in the long run. There is something a bit pathetic about recent attempts to make the old words seem modern by packaging them in contemporary media wrappings. As a character in a recent novel said, "I'm getting tired of hearing 'born again' words set to the rhythms of music meant for sex, drugs, and rock and roll."[4]

So, what *do* we do about our disconnection? I guess that depends on how we define the problem. I believe that we really are living in a kind of in-between time, a time between the death of older symbolic systems and the birth of new ones, between the death of the old metaphors of spiritual connectedness and the birth of a new language of faith appropriate to our modern consciousness. It would certainly seem that the traditional symbolic system we have known as Western Christianity is feeble and gasping for breath. In Europe, where a very small percentage of the population ever attend any kind of religious services, it is not hard to believe that we are living in the post-Christian era, as some have claimed. And the mainstream churches in the United States are not that much healthier (an article in the *Nashville Tennessean* reported that nationwide the Presbyterian Church alone lost 69,000 members in 2008[5]). Nor does the recent outburst of fundamentalist and evangelical fervor in the country seem to offer much more than a negative reaction to cultural change. The noise of their protestations sound awfully much like the voices of fear, and fear seldom got us anywhere that was positive. And it is not just traditional

Christianity that is in trouble. The radical backlash in the Muslim world in response to the new realities of modern life would suggest that the general spiritual unease we are feeling extends beyond Western Christendom to other cultures and other religious traditions as well. So, what does the future hold? If we are truly living in this in-between time what can we look forward to? What will replace the traditional forms and symbols, this "language of belief" that seems to many to have lost its validity? It would take a better prophet than I am to answer that, but whatever we do find in the future to invigorate our spirits will depend upon what we are looking for, and I do know that I, for one, am not looking to get *back* to anything. I am not looking for a second Reformation to revitalize the Church. I am not looking for some self-assured prophet of moral certainty to tell me what to believe, what is right and what is wrong, who is evil and who is good. I am not looking for someone else's answers. And I am not looking to some other religious tradition that seems new and different only because of its cultural strangeness to take the place of the one I grew up with.

I am looking for something new. I am waiting for a new connection. I am waiting expectantly for new metaphors to be born. I am looking today for something that probably will not come until tomorrow. I am looking to what I can see in the world around me to suggest to me a new way of imagining the world I cannot see. I am waiting for the Mystery to take a new shape. I am looking to the life of the world I know to give me a clue concerning whatever it is that transcends my temporal, physical existence. I am listening for the sound of my own breathing to harmonize with the respiration of the universe. I am feeling around in my life for a sense of where I am in history, for a sense of my place in the cosmos, in the natural world, and within the human family. I am looking, not for the assurance of some existence in the future, but for "heaven" to be realized in the love, joy, beauty, and wonder that I experience every day of my life in the world that is my present home. I believe that there will be a rebirth of wonder, and that there will arise new forms of connection with the Mystery that is the deeper truth about us. I do not know what shape those forms will take or when they will appear, but that is all right. For me, for now, it is enough to be waiting expectantly.

Would my father have understood anything of what I have been trying to say to him? Perhaps; perhaps not. It certainly would have been better had we been able to have this discussion face to face, had I been able to hear his questions and gauge his response to what I was trying to tell him. At least then there would have been a better chance for him to see that I had not just given up on everything I had believed, that what was important was not what I had lost, but what I was seeking. I hope that he might at least have seen my leaving the church as an embarkation on a serious journey and not just the result of some kind of moral or spiritual lapse. I doubt that he would ever have understood my need to let go of the traditional forms of religious belief in order to live in this "waiting period" in anticipation of the birth of something new. I think he could never have comprehended that the Church as he had known it and loved it would not last forever. We never had this discussion, of course; neither of us was ready for it. But what follows, though not addressed specifically to him, might, I suppose, be thought of as part of a dialogue that might have been.

Headbanging on Sacred Walls

*An upstart in the hallowed halls
of established religion*

When I was growing up it would never have occurred to me to ask whether or not the church my family attended was doing what the church was supposed to be doing. It would never have dawned on me that there might even be a question regarding the role of the church in society about which church members should concern themselves. The church was just the church doing the things that churches did. It was that building downtown where I went every week to Sunday school, morning worship, youth fellowship, Wednesday night prayer meeting, and the boy scouts, and it was as much a part of my life as Saturday night baths, the Sunday funny papers, and going to school the rest of the week. It was one of the places where I lived, and I have to say that I found a lot of good stuff there. It was where I met my best friend, Bill, when I was eleven and he was ten, both of us having just arrived in the "big city" from smaller towns in other states (a relationship that has defined for me the word "friend" for over six decades). It was where I met my first sweetheart, where I learned to sing in a choir and to love great music, and where I met caring and concerned adults from outside my immediate family who loved me and respected me. I was very fortunate that my church, the First Presbyterian Church of Birmingham, Alabama, was not in the business of indoctrinating young people with a lot of the negatives that churches sometimes teach. The kind of religion that I got there was, if somewhat benign and rather tame, at least positive and capable of growing. As far as I can recall, the emphasis of my early religious education was on what to be *for*, not on what to be *against*. Yes, the church was theologically conservative and culturally middle class. And, of course, it was segregated and lily white, but in those days, during and immediately following World War II, everything in the South was still segregated; the rumblings of change— at least as far as the white community was concerned—had not yet begun to be felt. But later on, when social change did come, I found that what I had learned there—especially under the tutelage of one liberal-spirited woman named Alice Scott Lowe, the church's education director—had effectively inoculated me against the fearful racism of my parents' generation. So, in spite of its shortcomings and its pretensions, the church was then, and remains in my memory of those times, a beloved institution to which I am indebted for many good things.

But my comfort level with that nice old establishment was about to be disturbed. The discomfort began, surprisingly, when I entered the theological seminary to study for my ordination to the ministry. Expecting the seminary to be merely a sort of postgraduate youth fellowship of earnest young men preparing to be leaders in the Presbyterian institution that I had always known (the "MBAs" of the business of religion?), what I found there was a ferment of ideas that posed for the first time a serious challenge to all of my long-held assumptions about what the Church was supposed to be and consequently what the minister's task was supposed to be. It was the mid-fifties, and a revolutionary breeze was wafting through the halls of American Protestant theological education. It was a quiet storm of new ideas in the writings of a group of men with German names: Karl Barth, Emil Brunner, Dietrich Bonhoeffer, Paul Tillich. All of these men had lived, studied, taught, or pastored in Germany during the twenties and thirties and had witnessed the rise of Nazism and the almost wholesale failure of the established churches to stand up to Hitler and the National Socialists' corruption of German society. Not only had the Christian community failed to resist, a large proportion of German Protestants had acquiesced in Hitler's call for a "German Christian" movement, which placed the swastika at the center of the cross and successfully recruited the support of the churches for Hitler's plans for a new and purer Germany. In 1934 a relatively small group of Lutheran and Reformed pastors, ministers, and professors who called themselves "Confessing Christians" signed *The Barmen Declaration* written mostly by Karl Barth[1], which declared their allegiance to God over the state and denounced Hitler's subversion of the Church. Among the signers was the Lutheran pastor Dietrich Bonhoeffer, whose stirring little book, *The Cost of Discipleship*[2] became standard reading in the seminary. He was later arrested and executed by the Nazis, accused of participating in a plot to assassinate Hitler. Paul Tillich had been dismissed from a teaching position at the University of Frankfurt because of his views in opposition to the Nazis. He moved to the United States and became a major new voice in American theological thought. Karl Barth, forced to leave Germany in 1935 after he refused to swear allegiance to Hitler, returned to his native Switzerland where he joined his friend and fellow theologian, Emil Brunner, in calling for a radical recommitment of the Church to the Christ of the New Testament. He taught until his death in 1968 at the University of Basle, and became perhaps the most important Protestant theologian of the middle years of the twentieth century.

I happened to arrive at the seminary just as the influence of these men and their ideas was beginning to be felt. Mind you, the urgent call for a renewal of the Church that was coming out of postwar Europe had not set the whole student body on fire with a revolutionary zeal, but for a significant number of the more thoughtful among us young "theologues," a new spark had been lit. Our studies took on an exciting intensity and our calling to the ministry a new depth of purpose. It wasn't so much that we became the avid disciples of any one of these particular men; we weren't "Barthians" or "Tillichians," and not many of us were all that eager to go to the extremes for our faith to which Bonhoeffer had gone. It was, rather, that the example of their experience with the Church in Europe, the courage of their commitment, and the clarity of their thought about the basic precepts of Christian belief stimulated in us what I would call a new kind of "theological seriousness." We were gripped by the need to take more seriously what it meant to be a Christian without focusing merely on an individual's personal "salvation." We felt that that kind of self-centered preoccupation was secondary to what it meant to be Christians in the world, what it meant to be the Church, a committed witnessing community of believers living out that commitment in a secular, materialistic society. That demanded a new clarity about the weekday implications of our Sunday professions of faith. It seemed to us that the Church was called to act in the world as something more than merely a kind of religious Elks or Kiwanis club, a nice organization for the socially and morally respectable among our citizens, and we were excited about what the Church could be. But we also had come to believe that intellectual laziness and "sloppy" theologizing on the part of its leaders had brought the teaching and preaching of mainstream American churches down too often to little more than a sort of watered-down cultural moralism. Telling people to "be good" was not the revolutionary New Testament message we believed we were called to proclaim. The churches in the South had grown soft and self-satisfied and safe, not unlike the churches of Europe in the days before Hitler's challenge. And we sensed that a time of testing was coming for us as well.

When my new classmates and I sat down for the first lecture of our first course in basic theology, we discovered that one of our fellow students was an older black man. There were no regularly enrolled African-American students in the seminary at that time, so at first we didn't know who he was or where he had come from. It turned out that he was the pastor of a local Baptist church who was auditing the course for his own continuing education. It also turned out that his name was the Reverend Dr. King, and that he was the father of another Dr. King who would become the main voice of the enormous challenge that would soon be facing us. By the time I graduated four years later, that challenge had become a very loud reality. I had already "received a call" (a pious euphemism for getting hired) in the middle of my senior year to become, upon graduation, the pastor of the Summerton Presbyterian Church in the small town of Summerton, South Carolina. Why did I choose to go to South Carolina? I guess it just seemed sort of natural; I was born there, I went to college there, my future wife Rebecca, was from there. It definitely was not because I saw in advance what I was getting into. Not long after I had made my decision, a good friend came to my dormitory room, handed me a little book, and said, "Lucius, you need to read this, especially chapter 2." The book, *The Deep South Says Never*, by John Bartlow Martin[3], consisted of a series of articles he had written on race relations in the South for the *Saturday Evening Post*. The second chapter was titled "Black Belt Town," and it was all about Summerton, South Carolina. I had known, of course, that race was a big issue there. But I did not know just *how* big. I had somehow missed the fact that in 1951 the first school desegregation case to reach the United States Supreme Court—which eventually resulted in the 1954 landmark decision declaring state sponsored school segregation unconstitutional—was *Briggs v. Elliot*, and Elliot was the chairman of the school board of Clarendon

County, South Carolina School District Number One. That was Summerton! And "Black Belt Town" was a detailed history of that case and of the recent dogged fight on the part of the town's leaders to preserve their little bastion of absolute white supremacy.[4] Three of the six persons cited by name in the chapter were current members of my church; a fourth was the late minister whom I was replacing. Most notable among those good Presbyterians was the school board's lawyer, Emory S. Rogers, who had argued the case before the Supreme Court against the NAACP's attorney, Thurgood Marshall. He was also the founder and executive director of the statewide association of White Citizens Councils of South Carolina (which were known by some as "the Klan in business suits"). I would never see Mr. Rogers in church while I was there—his ardent racism seemed to be the only religion he actively practiced—but he would play a major role in the story of my brief sojourn in Summerton. I wonder now, had I read Mr. Martin's little book before my "call" was received, if I would have gone there at all. But by then it didn't matter; I was committed. So, newly ordained at the age of twenty-six, armed with the hopeful enthusiasm of youth and my new "theological seriousness" about the Church, I found myself getting my professional feet wet in the forward trenches of the South's new "civil war."

I may have been young and idealistic and hampered by inexperience, but I was not a total fool. I knew that I was not going to walk into that town and start changing people's minds about race. When I was interviewed by the church's pulpit committee, I was asked about my views, and I made no effort to hide them. I told them that despite our differences, I would be willing to come be among them and work with them as their minister and listen to where they were coming from. But I made no promises about what I would or would not say or do about the issue of race, nor, to their credit, did they ask for such. In the time that I was there, I never preached a sermon on the subject of race relations. That would have amounted to pouring gasoline on a smoldering fire. They knew where I stood; I saw no need to beat them over the head with it. I judged it a better course to concentrate on being their pastor (and they needed one, for beneath the surface of their Southern gentility and manners, they were a troubled and anxious people). In time, by means of biblically based and theologically sound teaching and preaching on the basics of Christian belief, and by quiet example, I might hope gradually to inspire, in at least a few, a fresh vision of what the Church could be and how it could offer a new and more positive way of approaching the coming inevitability. My naiveté must have been as apparent as the wet behind my twenty-six-year-old ears.

Rebecca and I were welcomed with open arms. It must have been very exciting for the congregation to have newlyweds in the manse after thirty years of witnessing the slow decline in my predecessor's health and vitality and his wife's increasing reclusiveness. And I was certainly a breath of fresh air from the pulpit. It was a happy beginning for my first pastorate, and I was looking forward to good things happening there. Early on, I had decided that I should endeavor to establish some kind of relationship with the attorney, Emory Rogers, so, one afternoon that first summer I paid a call on him in his law offices upstairs over a downtown store. In his greeting he was the epitome of Southern charm and grace. I knew little more about him than what I had read in *The Deep South Says Never*, while he, no doubt, had all the intelligence on me, and our first encounter was something of a friendly sparring contest. I don't remember much of what we talked about that day but I do recall the phrase, "… human nature being what it is…" that kept coming up as a kind of cooly intellectual point of departure between us, as if to say: "If we could agree on that big question, we might just be able to find a common ground for discussion, but until then…" Well, at least, I thought, I had opened a dialogue with him, and for a time I continued on occasions to drop by for a friendly matching of wits. He was always charming, cool, and quick as a fox, and he never once lapsed into anything resembling a racist diatribe. Despite what I had read about him he didn't seem to be the ogre that the book had painted. After each such encounter I left feeling that I had held my own pretty well. Looking back now, I can imagine what *he* must have been feeling as I left: how long would it be before something would have to be done about this upstart young preacher? But he would bide his time.

The first two years of my tenure in Summerton passed rather routinely. Just the slightest hint of a potential rift between me and the congregation came when I made an attempt to get them into a closer connection with the larger Presbyterian family. The Presbyterian Church, U.S. (what was then the designation for the Southern branch of Presbyterianism) published a magazine from its headquarters in Richmond, Virginia, called the *Presbyterian Survey*, which contained news and articles about the church at large, and it offered to churches a subscription plan with a group rate for enrolling every family in a congregation. I thought that would be a good idea, and when I proposed it to the congregation's elders—even though I knew they were leery of "outsider" influence—they begrudgingly went along. I thought I had won a small victory, but after about the third monthly issue had been received, and while I was away on vacation, the elders met and voted to cancel the subscription. I think they didn't really want a confrontation with me; but they were making it plain what they thought of the "liberal propaganda" coming out of Richmond. I decided that there was no principle there to fight for that was worth the risk of my good standing with the congregation, so I let it drop. I did, however, dig in my heels over one issue. During the summer months the chairman of the church's property committee was in the practice of hiring a couple of African-American youngsters, twelve or thirteen years old, to mow the grass at the church and the manse. During my second spring I looked out one morning and found the two boys cranking up their mower to cut our front yard. The problem was that summer vacation had not begun and it was a school day. When I asked them what they were doing, they said that "Mr. Alec" had told them to come cut our grass. I asked them if they weren't supposed to be in school, and they said, "Well, yes sir, but Mr. Alec said…" I told them that it was okay for them to cut the grass on Saturday, but they couldn't skip school to do it, regardless of what Mr. Alec said, and I sent them away. I never heard from Mr. Alec on the matter, but I am sure that he took due note of my conviction that the school attendance of a couple of "colored boys" took precedence over his "white boss" authority. And I am sure that my act of interference was discussed in the unofficial councils of small town affairs. My one attempt to address the larger picture of race relations in the town was done under the cover of the U.S. Mail. I wrote to the Rev. E. E. Richburg, the minister who had been one of the leaders of the black community during their long struggle over school desegregation. I simply introduced myself as a fellow minister and expressed my hope that we would at some point be able to work together for the good of the community as a whole and invited him to contact me if I could ever be of any assistance to him. His reply was prompt and gratifying. He welcomed my overture and echoed my hope that we could work together in the future, and he closed by telling me that in all the years that he had been the pastor of the Liberty Hill A.M.E. Church, I was the first white minister in the community to initiate any contact with him as a fellow clergyman. Unfortunately, events were building that would prevent any follow up on our initial exchange of letters.

One day, some time during the spring of my third year in Summerton, I was totally surprised by a phone call from Emory Rogers inviting me to have lunch with him and his son-in-law. This had never happened before, and I wasn't sure what to make of it. I knew the son-in-law hardly at all, even though he was a member of my church (like his father-in-law, in name only). But I saw no reason to think that this was anything but a friendly gesture. We drove in the lawyer's big Cadillac to a popular restaurant in the nearby county seat town of Manning. Mr. Rogers, being a famous man in the county, was no doubt recognized by the restaurant staff as well as by many of the other patrons as we took our places at a table in the middle of the crowded dining room. The only thing I remember about the meal was that, at one point, he and I got into a rather heated discussion about something related to the issue of race. It didn't amount to much more than the kind of debates we had had in the privacy of his office, the difference being, of course, that this one took place in public and with a silent witness sitting at the table. Still, I felt no alarm since, like all our previous contests, the meeting ended on a pleasant and fairly cordial note. It was not until a week or two later that I learned that the very next morning after our lunch together, the attorney had walked into the drugstore on Main Street—which served as the town's unofficial, but very effective, communications center—and called out in a loud voice to one of my Presbyterian elders seated on the other side of a room full of coffee drinkers, "Well, what do you think of your nigger-lovin' preacher?"

I was only alerted that trouble was brewing when another of my elders—one who had become a trusted friend—called to tell me that we needed to talk. His name was Dickey Dingle (Dingle was almost as common a surname as Smith in that part of lower South Carolina; there were three families of Dingles in my small congregation. And Dickey was his real given name). Though he was not part of the old-money aristocracy that ran the town, he was one of the most respected men in the community, based solely on his fundamental honesty and integrity and the good-natured grace of his personality. With no formal education beyond high school, he made his living as an independent logger, harvesting pulpwood for a large paper mill that operated in a nearby county. He lived with his wife and six children in a large two-story frame house right off of Main Street that always seemed to need a paint job. I think that his keenest ambition in life must have been to serve his children as their good father, and for that job, he seemed particularly well equipped. If he was a plain man—in his lifestyle and personal habits—he was by no means a simple man. He was fully and painfully aware of the moral contradictions and the cultural anxieties that were being exposed as his community reacted to the oncoming racial revolution. And when he was as intensely serious as he was on the day he walked into my office, he demanded to be listened to, even by a hotshot young know-it-all of a Presbyterian minister.

He wasted no time in getting to the point of his visit: "Lucius, if you don't start watching your mouth, you are going to get into a lot of trouble." Then he related what had happened in the drugstore the day after my lunch with the attorney. Surely I should have known better, he told me, than to get into an argument with Emory Rogers, especially in public. At first I reacted to his warning as if he were telling me that I should compromise what I believed in, and that got my back up a little bit. What was I supposed to do, just roll over and play dead when I was directly challenged about something I believed in? And maybe it was time that the lawyer's son-in-law saw that not everyone was completely cowed by the old man. Dickey kept repeating that I had better be careful and that I didn't understand what I was dealing with, and he was growing increasingly frustrated over my failure to take his warning seriously. "Lucius," he said, interrupting one of my defensive protests, "let me ask you a question." The look on his face and the tone of his voice finally shut me up. "Do you know what it feels like to want to kill a man because he comes to your front door instead of your back door?" The silence between us was gelatinous.

"No," I said when I was able to reply, "I don't know what that feels like."

He nodded sadly, "I didn't think so. And until you *do* have some sense of what that is about, you will have no idea of the depth of the feelings and the power of the fears you are messing around with. Please...be careful what you say and who you say it to. I don't want you or your family to get hurt."

I left Summerton within a year of that conversation. I didn't leave because of any overt unpleasantness over my views on race. There were no threats, not even a hint of any disenchantment with me on the part of the congregation. No one came to tell me it was time for me to go. There had been no obvious repercussions from my public debate with Emory Rogers or from his even more public labeling of me. In fact, had it not been for Dickey Dingle's warning, I might never even have known that the drugstore incident had occurred. As far as I was aware nothing had changed...

except me. Dickey's piercing question had punctured my self-confidence. I wasn't sure of anything now, except that I was in over my head in a situation that I really didn't understand. I could see that there might be trouble ahead, though what form it would take was in no way apparent. I found myself very unsettled about what I should be doing with the new "ignorance" I had gained, and so began to rationalize the feeling that, perhaps, it was time to move on to "greener pastures." I let it out on the ministerial grapevine that I was available for a move, and when the second pulpit committee that came calling offered me a way out, I grabbed it. But my leaving Summerton the way I did left a scar on my conscience. I felt no real sense of accomplishment, or any obvious reason to throw in the towel when I did, only a vague notion that the commitment I had made to that congregation had not been fulfilled, that I wasn't finished there, that I should have stayed on longer. And I believe that the remainder of my time in the ministry was adversely colored by the nagging feeling that my very first opportunity to be the kind of minister that I had dreamed of being had ended in a cop out.

Looking back now, I was probably being unnecessarily hard on myself, although it took me almost fifty years to realize it. For some reason I had never gone back to reexamine the circumstances of that lunch with Emory Rogers. At the time, probably because I was already turning my attention toward leaving and because I never personally experienced—apart from Dickey's warning—any direct repercussions from it, I simply dismissed it as an unfortunate but rather minor lapse in judgment on my part. It was not until I began to write this chapter, and to relive that time in Summerton, that it finally dawned on me what that lunch had really been about. The attorney whose every breath was dedicated to the fight to preserve white supremacy in South Carolina did not just wake up one morning and think it would be a nice gesture to invite the young minister of his church to have lunch with him and his son-in-law. I am convinced now that he had decided that it was time to undercut whatever influence I might have gained in the town, and he knew exactly how to do it. He had already gotten me to spar with him in the privacy of his office. All he had to do was get me into a public debate in front of witnesses. He lured me into a trap, handed me a bit of rope by egging me into an argument, and I hanged myself. I would not be surprised if even the choice of the table in the center of the restaurant rather than a more private booth was carefully calculated for the most exposure to eavesdropping ears. But just to make sure that I would be heard spouting my "radical ideas" in public, he supplied his own witness; his son-in-law was present, I now believe, merely to listen and to corroborate his father-in-law's version of my public exposure. And as soon as he made his pronouncement to the drugstore crowd, my ministry in that town was damaged beyond repair. He had tagged me with the two words that turned me instantly into an outsider. While those two words were enough to do the job on me, I doubt that they were all he had to say; I suspect he took his time relating to anyone who would listen his own embellished version of how I abused his hospitality by verbally challenging his beliefs, or something to that effect. I wonder if he took his "witness" along for coffee that morning.

Of course I was never supposed to know that the white letters standing for n____r-lover had, as it were, been painted on my back for the whole town to see. There was a conspiracy of silence that reigned over the town of Summerton. There were secrets that everyone knew but that no one would acknowledge openly—like the fact that a number of the white businesses on Main Street were businesses in name only. With virtually no customers, they were simply propped up by some kind of economic hocus-pocus invented by the town's powerful elite to ensure that no white business would be allowed to fail. Their owners complied with the charade by going to "work" every day and sitting around doing virtually nothing. So, likewise, everybody in town would know about my branding, except me and my wife. And no one came forward to tell me that I was in trouble…not my neighbor down the street, a deacon in the church, who took me fishing for striped bass on Lake Marion; not the young business man who had chaired the committee that had "called" me to Summerton, with whose wife and family I had sat for hours in a hospital waiting room in Charleston while he underwent brain surgery; not the bank president, with whom I had watched and waited and prayed as his aged father took his final breaths; not the mayor of the town, with whom I agonized over his son's alcoholism; not the grocery store owner and his wife who graciously took me out to Sunday dinner while my wife was in the hospital with our first child; not the retired Navy Commander, a voracious reader, who shared his love of books with me; not the parents whose children I had baptized; nor the loved ones of those whose funerals I had conducted; nor the mothers and fathers at whose sons' and daughters' weddings I had officiated. Only one man, one courageously caring man, dared to break the silence. Not that anything threatening to life or limb would have happened, nothing like that. No rocks would have been thrown, no crosses burned; they didn't allow the Klan to operate in Clarendon County. I would simply have been frozen out, ignored, made irrelevant, until I left of my own accord, which—in shorter time than they expected—is exactly what happened. I had no need to feel guilty over leaving when I did. It didn't really matter whether I left sooner or later; it was all the same to those who had made the decision that I was no longer a factor in the life of their town.

About four years after I left Summerton, and more than a decade after the Supreme Court had ordered the states to proceed with "all deliberate speed" to dismantle the system of segregated public education, Clarendon County School District Number One was finally forced to comply. Even then, in the fall of 1965, only the token integration of a few black students into the formerly all-white elementary and high schools took place. At the same time, the white flight from the public schools had also begun, facilitated by the establishment of a new private school founded by and temporarily housed in the Summerton Baptist Church. Not that the impetus for opening the new school came solely from the Baptists. They just had the largest building. I am sure that the majority of Presbyterians, Methodists, and

Episcopalians joined with them in the effort to ensure that education in the district would remain segregated by race. In time, the funds would be found for the new campus of what would become Clarendon Hall, a private "Christian" school, and by 1970, when the U.S. Court of Appeals for the Fourth Circuit mandated complete desegregation, almost all white students had left the public schools to enroll in the new all-white academy. Back in the 1950s when Emory Rogers was actively fighting tooth and nail to preserve segregation, he boasted once that it would be the twenty-first century before the white children of Summerton would go to school with negro children. I doubt that even he could have believed back then how accurate his prophecy would turn out to be. As recently as 2004, school enrollment in Summerton remained, to all intents and purposes, divided along racial lines. Nearly all of the white kids attend the private Clarendon Hall, leaving the public schools almost entirely African-American. And as if in testimony to the truth that "separate" can never be "equal," the standardized achievement test scores for the public "black" schools of the district were among the lowest in the state.

If by getting out of Summerton I expected to leave my troubles behind, I was sadly mistaken. Whereas Summerton had only begun to feel like the proverbial frying pan heating up under me, my move to the town of Mullins, South Carolina, was a masochistic leap into the fire. I still shake my head in bewilderment at my decision to go there. Never have I lived anywhere for any length of time (I was there for three years) where I felt so completely out of place.

My formal, "backward-collar," high church, theologically
serious Presbyterianism made me an alien in a culture totally
dominated by a Southern Baptist salvationist religion that
seemed to me to be based more upon sentiment than upon
sound theological or biblical thinking (and over half of my
Presbyterian congregation were expatriate Baptists!). The
economic wealth of the town consisted largely of recently
garnered tobacco money (Mullins was the country's seventh
largest tobacco market), which left the well-to-do with a kind
of "nouveau riche" insecurity, in contrast to the old cotton-
plantation, inherited wealth of Clarendon County. Also
in contrast to Clarendon County, the resistance to social
change on the part of the citizens of Mullins was marked by
a definite Klan mentality. Toward the end of my troubled
tenure there, I would have occasion to experience personally
and up close a very frightening expression of that barbarous
mindset (more about that in a later chapter).

After departing Mullins under pressure, and following a sabbati-
cal year of postgraduate study at the Louisville Presbyterian
Seminary in Louisville, Kentucky, I arrived in Nashville to
take up the post of Associate Minister to the large (2,000-
plus member) congregation of the Westminster Presbyterian
Church. I thought that I had finally come home. Enough of
small towns in the rural South; that was not where I belonged.
After all, I had grown up in a big city downtown church
with a well-educated and cultured congregation, and I
believed that Nashville was where I could finally be the kind

of minister I thought I should be. And to a degree that was true. The church was large enough to include a significant minority of liberal, forward-looking people, and during my time there we did some exciting things having to do with religion and the arts, and with new experimental forms of ministry (foremost among them was a very successful—if controversial—coffee house ministry to the youth of the city). About a year after I had joined the staff, the church's senior minister retired, and to succeed him, the congregation called the Reverend Daniel Patrick McGeachy III. "Pat" was only three-and-a-half years my senior, and he and I had gotten to know each other several years earlier when we worked together briefly at a church youth conference in the mountains of North Carolina. I could not have been happier about the congregation's choice of a man to lead them in this challenging time of change, nor more delighted about the prospect of working with him again. And his arrival did have an impact. A thoughtful theologian and a powerful preacher with a warm, fun loving sense of humor and a definite flair for the dramatic, Pat brought to that staid old church a vitality it hadn't known for years. We both felt we were justified in our expectations of the great things that could be accomplished there.

But the times, they really *were* a-changin'! It was the tumultuous sixties, and revolution was in the air. The whole country seemed to be tearing itself apart. If the civil rights movement, with its sit-ins and marches and demands for desegregation, racial justice, and Black Power, had not been unsettling enough for middle-class white America, now came the hippies, the drug culture, the sexual revolution, the don't-trust-anyone-over-thirty generation gap, Woodstock, and rock and roll. And then there was Vietnam. For many who had lived proudly through our patriotic war against totalitarian Germany and Japan, then dutifully marched off to Korea to fight the Communists, and who had been raised on the Red Scare hysteria of McCarthyism, it must have been singularly disturbing to see American young people demonstrating against their country, burning their draft cards, and fleeing their homeland to avoid going to war. And in the midst of all of this, Pat and I thought we were going to introduce this quintessentially middle-class congregation of socially respectable and economically successful Presbyterians to *new* approaches to worship and *new* ways of interpreting the New Testament Gospel and *new* patterns for being the Church in the world? Just who were we fooling? The great majority of the people in those pews were not looking for anything new and exciting; in their anxiety over the current social upheavals, they were looking for something safe and familiar. Both of us, I think, came to feel a damaging disappointment at our failure to overcome the resistance that we seemed to meet at almost every turn, and for me it was a disappointment that was beginning to erode the dream that had led me into the ministry in the first place. I had never fully recovered from the trauma of my ouster from the church in Mullins, and already the intellectual problems with the faith, which I wrote about in the first chapter, had begun to gnaw at me. Somehow the whole decade between 1958 and 1968, which began so auspiciously for me personally with my ordination to the ministry, and for the country with the election of President John F. Kennedy and the promises of civil rights gains, had spiraled down to become pretty much a time for the death of dreams

Late on the afternoon of April 4, 1968, I was standing with a group of men in a downstairs corridor of Westminster Church. We were waiting outside the church fellowship hall while the final preparations were being made for a joint dinner meeting of the congregation's elders and deacons, when our conversation was interrupted by the loud voice of a late arrival: "Did y'all hear the news? Somebody shot Martin Luther King today in Memphis." The only reaction to that devastating announcement that I recall were the words of the person standing next to me, a young business man who had recently been elected and ordained as a deacon in the church: "Well, I hope whoever shot him had good aim!" If there was any other response to the news, I didn't hear it. In fact those words are the only thing I remember about that evening. It was not that I was so shocked by the callousness of that young church officer's hope for the shooter's success. The truth was that I was not shocked or surprised at all, and that was precisely the source of the despair I felt—that it was what I might have expected to hear—and that was what made those words the backbreaking straw laid upon my already burdened ministerial career. I think I knew in that exact moment that it was over for me; the only thing that remained was to decide what to do next with my life.

Looking back now, it is painful to consider just how completely we failed to accomplish what we set out to achieve, all of us earnest young men who went out from all those seminaries back in the1950s determined to change the Church. We really believed that it was possible for the Church to become an agency for the realization of a new era of social justice in the land. We believed it because we believed that such a mission was mandated by the Christian Gospel, the good news of God's unconditional love for all of his children. We believed it because we believed that to accept God's love was to accept our equality as brothers and sisters with all of those whom he also loves. It was as simple as that. And many of us—especially those who elected to serve in the Deep South—risked life and limb, as well as our professional futures, for that commitment. While it is impossible to measure the extent of our influence on individuals whose minds and attitudes may well have been changed forever by our witness, it seems pretty clear in retrospect that as far as our impact on the institutional Church was concerned, we might as well have been banging our bare heads on the walls of some ancient cathedral in a vain attempt to move it over just a bit. For all the earnestness of our efforts, it would seem that we accomplished very little. Over a half-century later the mainline Protestant churches continue, along with the country clubs, to be among the most brightly white establishments in America. And not only did the white churches fail to answer the call to take the lead in the struggle for racial justice, they allowed themselves to be used as one of the primary agencies in the racist strategy to deny the African-American dream of social, political, and economic equality. The most effective tool in the resistance to school desegregation in the south was not the Klan or the

White Citizens Councils but the "segregation academies," all-white private "Christian" schools like Clarendon Hall, founded by white Protestant churches. It would appear that in our belief that the Church could and should be a prime instrument for healing the wounds left over from slavery, we were about as far off base as we could have been. Why was that? Why, in fact, did so much of American Christendom, when confronted, as were the German churches before World War II, by the most right wing, reactionary elements in society, choose so often to throw its weight behind a movement to deny a whole people their basic human rights?

I believe that the answers to those questions have to do with the very nature of institutional religion. Over the years I've heard a lot of complaints about organized religion, or the institutional Church, mostly from people who are vaguely disenchanted with popular religion or resentful about some of the claims that the Church makes for itself. Those complaints seem usually to be a kind of unexamined, catchall grievance without many specifics as to what it is exactly that makes religion a problem when it is "organized" or "institutionalized." There is obviously nothing wrong with institutions as such. On the contrary, they are how we humans get things done. Any group of people who get together and organize themselves for the accomplishment of any specific purpose is, by definition, an institution in the making. Without organization and the creation of structures designed to enable people to work as a group to achieve the goals that brought them together in the first place, nothing gets done. So why does the word *Institution*, or the notion of being *organized*, have such negative connotations when used in association with religious belief?

In her book, *Beyond Belief,* Elaine Pagels writes about the consequences of the early Christian Church's efforts to establish itself—to get organized—during the centuries immediately following the crucifixion of Jesus.[5] During this time it seems that there were many different interpretations of his teaching and of the significance of his life and death being circulated. The writings we now know as the four New Testament Gospels were not the only versions of the life and teachings of Jesus being put forward by those who had either known him personally or had known his closest followers. Some of those writings took very different views than those of the authors of *Matthew, Mark, Luke,* and *John.* It was felt early on by the leaders of this new movement that its future was threatened by the controversies that were being sparked by these differing interpretations. So, councils were called to determine once and for all which of these writings were to be considered true and which were to be considered false. Thus, the "canon" of the New Testament, the official list of "books" to be included in what the Church would put forward as "The Word of God," was decided upon by men of the Church whose primary purpose was to ensure the future of the institution. Those other books were branded as "heretical," and their use by believers was officially banned. Many of them were no doubt destroyed and lost forever, but some of these lost Gospels have been rediscovered in recent years and are offering interesting insights into the earliest responses to the life and teachings of Jesus.

It was also during this period that the Church felt it was necessary to settle on a concise statement of belief that would contain the "correct" interpretation of the significance of Jesus' life and death in order to root out those alternative versions that were believed to be threatening the peace and stability of this new young organization (we mustn't have any free thinkers mucking up the works!). The result was the adoption in the fourth century of the Nicene Creed, which soon became part of the liturgy of the Church and is still recognized by many as an orthodox statement of Christian Church doctrine. So, it would seem that, from the earliest chapters of the story of Christianity, it was the aim of the men who were its leaders to domesticate and dampen, if not extinguish entirely, the blazing fires of personal inspiration in response to the teachings of Jesus. For the sake of the peace and stability of the Church, the insight and inspiration of the individual must be subordinate to the accepted (or imposed) belief of the community as a whole. And what is important to understand here is that this was not some nefarious scheme, as some conspiracy theorists would have us believe. Neither the establishment of the official canon of the New Testament nor the adoption of an official set of beliefs nor any of the various organizing strategies of the early church fathers came about because they were simply a bunch of power-hungry (male?) authority figures. There no doubt were some of those among them, but for the most part they were simply the leaders of a new institution that was doing exactly what every human institution does.

As with any organism, from the simplest one-celled amoeba to the most advanced animal, any established human organization, from the smallest to the largest, has a built-in instinct for self preservation. Institutions are inherently conservative and self-protective. An institution, regardless of its stated mission, does not, will not, cannot believe in self-sacrifice as an institutional strategy. The Church may preach self-sacrifice as a righteous goal for the individual, but it cannot practice it as a group enterprise (when an established organization *does* commit a group act of self-sacrifice—such as happened in the mass suicide at Jonestown—we consider that to be an act of some kind of hysteria, and rightly so). A normal human institution cannot be expected to act in ways that run counter to its basic instinct for survival. Toward the end of my time at Westminster Church, two of the prominent elders of the congregation came to see me to tell me that they thought it was time for me to leave. They were respectful and, I felt, even friendly toward me as a person. Nevertheless, they believed that I was, as one of them put it, "tearing up the church." How could that have been true? I wasn't that important. I wasn't even the senior minister. I preached only on rare occasions, led some study groups and worked with the young people. How could I be "tearing up" this long-established historic church? But they were right, even if they somewhat overstated their case. From the point of view of those two elders, both community leaders, one a prominent physician and the other a very successful businessman, who had been elected and solemnly ordained to shepherd this congregation through a difficult time of social upheaval, I was a source of irritation and controversy. I just seemed always—by what I said from the pulpit, by what I taught about Christian belief, by the kinds of things I tried get people involved with, by my very demeanor—to be raising questions that made people uncomfortable. Like the time I thought it appropriate to include homosexuals among those we should pray for during the eleven o'clock worship on Sunday. Mind you, this was before the word *gay* had come into use and before *those* kinds of people were even mentioned in polite company. One angry parishioner protested that it was no longer possible to discuss the morning service with his children over the Sunday dinner table. The coffee house ministry that I mentioned earlier was a constant source of irritation for a lot of people who just couldn't understand why the church should be involved with such a seemingly unreligious activity, and I was one of its founders. Those two elders knew, just as the early Church fathers did, that controversy is trouble for an organization with a voluntary membership. They knew that people who are upset and uncomfortable might just opt to stay away. They might even withdraw their financial support, heaven forbid, for everyone knows that money is the life blood of any institution that has buildings and grounds and expensive equipment (in this case a magnificent pipe organ) to maintain, and the salaries of a dozen or more staff members to pay. There simply was no comfortable place for someone like me—a "hacker of the underbrush," as a colleague once called me—on the payroll of such a staid and conventional establishment.

The reason we failed— we "theologically serious" young men who went out into the Church with a determination to turn it into a redemptive community for the healing of racial divisions—was that we just didn't understand the nature of the institution we were dealing with. We thought that the Church, because it was supposed to be about God, because it talked about God all the time and claimed, therefore, to be unique, was also supposed to behave differently from other institutions in society. And we were wrong about that. We simply weren't prepared for the reality that an institution is an institution, whether it be a church or a bank or a university or an insurance company or a restaurant chain, and so long as it is made up of human beings it will act like a human institution, no matter how different it claims to be. It was simply too much to expect that, in the name of some inspired sense of racial justice, any church—Protestant or Catholic, liberal or conservative—was going to risk its well-established existence as a useful and successful organization to go against the tide of prevailing social opinion and practice. Except in very rare instances, it simply wasn't going to happen, just as it wasn't going to happen during the thirties that the mainstream popular religious institutions in Germany would risk their status in society by standing up to Hitler. I don't know that those theologians and pastors who signed the *Barmen Declaration* really expected that kind of resistance to occur, but if they did they were about as far off-base as their young American followers of the fifties and sixties.

I must admit that, to this day, my feelings toward the Church are pretty ambivalent. I still love it for what it was to me in my youth. It was my home-away-from-home; its members were my extended family. The nurture I received there confirmed some parts of what I learned at home and, to my benefit, counteracted others. Considering the Church's reputation for indoctrination and close-mindedness, I suppose my early experience with it was unusual. For the most part, what it provided was a kind of elementary school for spiritual growth. It gave me the basic intellectual tools for asking and thinking about the deep questions of my humanness and, perhaps the biggest gift of all, it taught me how to keep an open mind. When I "graduated" from its school, I went off to get a higher education and to prepare to serve it for the rest of my life. Upon my return—with my new robes of office and my freshly honed theology—I found that the world the Church and I had known in my youth was changed. And when I thought to tell the Church that it, too, needed to change, it said to me, in effect, "Go away, son, and leave me be." And I finally got the message that I wasn't wanted in that place any longer, that it wasn't any longer my home, and I went away. I left with relief at my freedom from it, and some anger at its rebuff. That delicious sense of freedom remains. The anger has matured into something like a grown-up's nostalgia for old times that truly were good times, but can never be again.

Looking back now—from my ecclesiastical expatriate's vantage point—it seems to me that the main problem with organized religion is the clash between *religion* and *spirituality*. Someone has defined *spirituality* as "a personal response to the mystery of the world." The key word here is "personal." *Spirituality* has to do with the individual. It is the word we use to describe the singular person's unique sense of self in relation to the universe. It is found in the courage of a singular individual to stand alone outside the warm haven of conventional wisdom and allow the universe to ask him difficult questions about what he's doing here. It is being an open-eyed adult still living with the unformulated excitement of an innocently inquisitive child. *Spirituality* lies

...in the wonder that is a precursor to belief...

...in the questions that are the precursors to faith...

...in the curiosity that is the precursor to knowing...

...in the awe that is a precursor to understanding...

...in the silence that is the precursor to having something definite to say...

...in the searching that is the precursor to having a clear direction...

And always it lies in the primacy for me of *my* questions over *someone else's* answers.

On the other hand, I think of *Religion* as *domesticated* spirituality, institutionalized inspiration, group faith, shared belief. It is what happens when a number of people, by mutual consent, having agreed upon a common object of religious concern, come together to express that concern in an organized fashion. It occurs when a number of like-minded people have settled on what they are willing to say that they hold in common. It may be tightly or loosely defined—by general creeds, by specific beliefs, by a shared story of origins, or simply by a form of "common worship"—but to some extent it must grow out of consensus. In most cases those beliefs and stories and forms are not original to the present-day religious communities or their individual members. They were handed down from past generations, passed on and accepted virtually intact by contemporary adherents. They came down from yesterday's higher authority; they did not rise up out of the burning questions of today's spiritually searching individuals. *Religion* is comfortable; you know where it's going because you know where it's been. *Spirituality*, the persistent questioning of the seeking individual, is not comfortable; it has no tradition and you don't know where it might lead. From the point of view of institutional religion, individual spirituality can be downright dangerous; it's too loose because it's too personal. It tends to be revolutionary, and, as I know from personal experience, traditional establishments really don't tolerate well the individual who insists on asking troubling questions.

I believe, as I suggested in the first chapter, that we are living in a sort of "in-between time." It is an age of spiritual *angst* brought about by the death and decay of the traditional symbols and the language of belief, with the resulting failure of the established religious institutions to respond to the shifting boundaries of modern life in ways other than negative reaction or retreat into timeworn formulas. If this is so, then perhaps it is to those very "troubling questions" that we need to be listening. Neither the Church, the Synagogue, the Mosque, nor any of the traditional religious institutions, with their domesticated, handed-down ways of thinking and talking about belief, are capable of addressing the critical modern thirst for new metaphors of connection. Just as it was unrealistic for us young "headbangers" to expect the Church to become the agent for the healing of racism in America, so it would be foolish to expect the traditional religious establishments to even address the need for a new language of belief. They can't do that because it would mean that they would have to question the very words and creeds and formulations on which their common consensus of belief is based. And that would be tantamount to institutional suicide. This is not to say that the Church is so saddled with convention that it is not capable of doing good things. It is and does, especially in the realm of benevolent service. When organized groups of people really believe that their creator has called them to serve those in need, they can be a powerful force for good in the world. And in an overpopulated, depersonalized, and lonely world, the religious institution is one of the few places where people can find a community to which belonging is a matter of simple unconditional acceptance. It might even be possible that the Church could become the kind of elementary school for spiritual growth that I found it to be in my youth, if only it would pay more attention to the real questions of its members than to its own preconceived answers regarding morality and faith. But that can be a risky business.

I also suggested in the first chapter that, for me, this seems to be a time for waiting. I don't believe that the birth of the fresh metaphors that will connect me in a new way to the mystery of my own being can be rushed. So I come down, for now, on the side of *Spirituality* as opposed to *Religion*, on the side of personal questioning as opposed to the consensus of common faith. For the present and for the unforeseeable future, I think I just need to be patient and listen to the difficult questions that the universe asks me about my existence. I just need to put belief on hold for a while. But, in the meantime, I am not just sitting around hoping for something to happen. I am not, in the words of W. H. Auden, being ". . . held waiting in a packed lounge for a personal call from long distance, for the low voice that defines one's future."[6] I don't believe there will be any "personal calls from long distance"; there will be no outside voice, low or loud, that will define my future faith. There are many voices that shout loudly in my ear, "God, God, God!" but the urgency of their shouting sounds more like the desperate pleading of the lost and confused than a calm voice that I should follow out of my own temporary shadows. So, I choose to wait in the absence of certainty, but not just idly standing around in a state of spiritual paralysis wishing for someone to show me the light. I wait, rather, with an expectancy of new meaning.

I wait, for instance, next to a stream I have found flowing through a remote wooded area of a Tennessee State Park on a weekday when no one else is around. I wait for the clean, clear water that burbles softly over a course littered with the fractured remains of ancient rocks to hum to me a quiet song of my connection to the earth. Across the stream from where I wait, a sheer wall leaps upward out of the water that has labored for a million years to expose its face. And it is a living, changing face. Just above the surface of the stream, the water's most recent work is exposed in gray horizontal layers of limestone, laid down by the offerings of countless forgotten creatures from long forgotten seas who gave up their exoskeletons to provide for us, their inheritors, a solid place to stand. As my eyes climb upward, this sacrificial work is already being softened by a cloak of mosses and other miniscule plant forms that are taking root in the damp crevices of the rock. And the farther up I look, the larger the plants become, until the rock is hidden altogether. There are whole trees now that seem to have leaped out from between the wrinkles in the face with a determination to head due west, parallel to the ground below, until they realized the life-source of the sun was up and they turned toward it. At the top of the bluff the trees are the oldest, even though the rocks immediately beneath them are the youngest. It was up there that the stream began so long ago to patiently wear its way down through the layers of time. And I am suddenly aware that that is what I am looking at: not just a beautiful natural scene, but a picture of time. The stream and the living wall of rock that it has exposed form a snapshot of the eons that stretch back in one continuous unfolding, from this pleasant weekday afternoon all the way to the morning of the earth's formation. And I am no longer merely a detached onlooker, but a participant in this scene. This is *my* life story; this stream, these rocks are part of my genealogy. And I am overcome by a sense of the vital connection between me in this moment and whatever power or process gave the earth its being. I don't know how to say what this is, or what it means; my sense of connection has not yet gelled into metaphors that sum up what I sense to be true. For now, I will just have to wait in the expectancy that meaning will come.

From this kind of experience—when I have listened to the testimony of a stream, or from other such quiet responses to nature and relationships and events in the world around me—has grown a deeper and deeper conviction that the "meaning" that I seek will be found, not in any kind of "answers" to any sorts of presupposed "religious questions," but rather in that sense of connection I felt in the moment described above. And I dare to believe that this is what all of us want and need more than anything else. More than answers, more than specific beliefs about our origins and our destinies, I believe we want and need a sense of connection. More than anything else we are, in the words of the old folk tune, "...just a'lookin' for a home, just a'lookin' for a home." It is that longing for connection, that need for a "home" in the universe, in the natural world, and in the human family that I believe we are really seeking.

TRUTH IS WHERE YOU FIND IT

All truth is sacred,
all books are human

THE BIBLE WAS THE FIRST BOOK that I was introduced to as a very young child; not the Bible itself, of course, but the book of Bible stories that my mother regularly read to me. If there were any other children's books in our home, I don't recall them, only that thick blue volume with all the strange pictures that also became my first introduction to art. We were not a literary family at all; our home contained very few books of any kind. Neither of my parents were regular readers. My mother did like poetry, though her unsophisticated taste ran mostly to the likes of Edgar A. Guest's sentimental doggerel and the frontier ballads of Robert Service. She must have read the rhymes of Mother Goose to me because I seem always to have known about the nonsense prompted by the "Cat and the Fiddle," the dietary accommodations of "Jack Spratt" and his wife, and the shenanigans of "Old Mother Hubbard" and her poor dog. But that Bible storybook was the main course in my early home pre-schooling.

My interest in those stories was not particularly religious. Like any young child, I liked a good story full of adventure, with heroes and villains and suspense, with enough strange goings on to stimulate my imagination and whet my curiosity.

And how could you beat a tale of a man being thrown overboard from an ancient sailing ship by his enemies, being swallowed up by a whale, and then being spit out safely on a distant shore? When I later saw Walt Disney's *Pinocchio* and the boy/puppet got swallowed by a whale, that story was already familiar to me. Or what about the story of a young boy who is so loved by his mother that she makes him a beautiful coat of many colors, only to have his jealous brothers steal his coat and throw him in a deep pit to die, who then gets rescued by strangers and carried off to a foreign country where he gains the favor of the king and gets to be one of the king's principal advisors? That's a Cinderella story for boys. And then there's the one about a young lad who is called upon by his people to defend them against their enemies' champion fighter, who happens to be a giant named Goliath. Refusing to put on armor and carry a sword, he declares that he will depend upon his trusty slingshot, whereupon he hits that giant right between the eyes with a rock large enough to knock him dead, and his people are saved! If that's not *Adventure Comics* material, I don't know what is. Of course, my mother thought that she was working on my religious education when she was filling my head with all these "biblical" stories; little did she know that she was mainly whetting my future appetite for cowboy movies and comic books.

Of course, there was a lot of religious stuff in the book, too. There were stories about people worshipping the wrong gods and being defeated in battle by the good guys who worshipped the real God (I didn't know what it meant "to worship"). There was a lot of stuff about the Israelites—the good guys—praying and causing God to do magical things like parting seas, making water flow out of a rock, causing some kind of food called manna to fall out of the sky, the sun to stand still, and the walls of a whole city (belonging to the bad guys) to fall down. There was one particularly religious story that I remember, especially because it was illustrated with a colored picture that fascinated me and is engraved upon my visual memory to this day. It was the story of Jacob's Ladder, Jacob's dream of a great ladder reaching up to heaven with all of these angels "ascending and descending" (I never could figure out how they could go in both directions at the same time on one ladder). I had no idea what that story was about, and I still don't, but I loved that picture with its dark blue sky over the tiny sleeping figure of Jacob, and that long ladder with ephemeral winged figures disappearing into the thick clouds at the top of the page. I figured heaven must be somewhere up there in the clouds at the top of the page. But there was one religious story in the book whose message was very clear to me. It was the one story that seemed to speak to me personally about the nature of God and about my relationship with Him. It is the story that I remember most clearly of all the ones that my mother read to me: the one about the children and the bears.

As I recall, it went like this: There was this old "prophet" (?) named Elisha, who was walking along out in the countryside one day when some children ran after him and began to mock him. I didn't know precisely what it meant to "mock" someone, but I gathered that it wasn't a nice thing to do, especially since Elisha was a man of God. Children aren't supposed to make fun of holy things, and Elisha was very angry at them. Being a man of God, he was able to make things happen, so he called some bears out of the woods and they came and ate up the bad children. Now there was a message for an impressionable little boy: you'd better behave yourself and watch your language, or God will get you. As it turns out, the story as it is told in the real Bible is even scarier:

> *"He (Elisha) went up from there to Bethel; and while he was going up on the way, some small boys came out of the city and jeered at him, saying, 'Go up, you bald head! Go up, you bald head!' And he turned around, and when he saw them, he cursed them in the name of the Lord. And two she-bears came out of the woods and tore forty-two of the boys."*
> (2 Kings 2: 23–24, RSV)

Forty-two of them! Man alive, "jeering" at one of God's prophets and calling him an "old bald head" must be an awful sin to make God *that* mad! (Or is it that God just doesn't like city boys?). Was I really supposed to believe that story? I guess I was. After all, it was in the Bible, and the Bible, of course was all true. My mother must have read the story to me more than once to get the point across. I sure remembered it. And even today I sort of tremble at the message it conveys.

In 1935 in Boston, the great American musical composer, George Gershwin, premiered his opera *Porgy and Bess*, based

Truth Is Where You Find It

on a story written by a distant (immeasurably distant) cousin of mine, DuBose Heyward, about African-American life in Charleston, South Carolina.[1] In the second act, he has one of his characters, a dope dealer named Sportin' Life sing a surprisingly cynical—surprising for the place and times—commentary on religion, which begins:

> *"It ain't necessarily so;*
> *It ain't necessarily so;*
> *The things that you're liable*
> *To read in the Bible;*
> *It ain't necessarily so…"*

In later years, I remember my mother, on hearing that song played on the radio, being righteously incensed that anyone would dare to make fun of so precious a truth as the infallibility of the Bible as the word of God. If she could have, she probably would have called out some of those she-bears to chew on old Sportin' Life.

One of the key foundation stones of each of the three dominant religions of the West—Judaism, Christianity, and Islam—has been the belief that the ultimate truths that form the core teachings of each are to be found in the pages of their sacred scriptures: the Old Testament, the New Testament, and the Koran, respectively. These writings, believed to be divinely inspired, represent the final authority for believers in all matters of faith and life, and much of the activity that makes up the life of the religious communities of each of these major bodies of faith is centered on the study and interpretation of these holy writings. So honored are they, considered as they are by many believers to have been practically dictated by the deity himself, that in all three religions, the books themselves have become objects of veneration. Hence, to my mother it was blasphemous that anyone should suggest, especially in such a ribald ditty sung by, of all people, a dope dealer, that what one reads in the Bible "...ain't necessarily so." To question the infallibility of the "Holy Book" was to undercut the very authority on which religious faith is based.

The persistent need for some outside authority in spiritual matters has created a lot of problems over the centuries, especially when that authority has been vested in a powerful individual or a group of powerful persons. Lord Acton's oft quoted assertion that "power corrupts and absolute power corrupts absolutely" was never more relevant than when it refers to the temptation incurred by one who has assumed the role of direct representative of an omnipotent divine being. We hardly need remind ourselves of historic examples of this kind of corruption, from the high priests of ancient times who vied with kings and pharaohs for control of their peoples, through the multitudes of preachers and priests who have used their power as "holy men" to line their pockets and extend their influence into realms beyond the spiritual, to the recent sordid revelations of Catholic priests who employ their spiritual influence to gain sexual dominance over children. And who can forget the bizarre scene of hundreds of people lining up to drink poisoned Kool-Aid at the behest of their spiritual leader, the infamous Jim Jones. Somehow, people who hunger after spiritual reassurance seem singularly vulnerable before the persuasion of a leader whom they have been convinced has some special connection to the Almighty. But the power of authority to corrupt spiritual life is a danger not only when that authority is vested in persons, but also when it is believed to reside in the pages of an infallible, "sacred" book. We have witnessed only too clearly in the opening years of the twenty-first century the corrosive fallout of religious fundamentalism, the troubles that can occur when a sizable number of people in a society are seduced into believing that the final truth about life is fixed and unchanging, and that that one truth is contained in the pages of a "holy book."

I first encountered reactionary religious fundamentalism "up close and personal" as a young theological student back in the fifties. Oh, I had grown up with the kind of benign fundamentalism that was practiced by my parents. They, like many others of their generation, and like many today, had simply bought into the whole Protestant Church thing. As far as I can remember they evidenced no really deeply personal religious convictions; they were just Presbyterians. They went to church regularly, were active in its programs, supported it financially, and accepted its teachings without question. That included the belief that the Bible was the inerrant Word of God. But they avoided any kind of extremism like the plague; such things were just not in their makeup. My mother might turn off the radio when Sportin' Life started singing his cynical parody on the Bible, but she wasn't about to go to war with anyone about it. Belief in the

Bible was just part of the package she accepted, that's all. She didn't have much time for those who "went off the deep end" about such questions.

That was the way I was brought up and how my religious convictions were shaped until I enrolled in the theological seminary to begin preparing for a nice, safe career as a mainstream Presbyterian minister. I had graduated from the social and religious comfort of the Church's youth fellowship into the equally benign atmosphere of a small church college where for four years nothing I had learned in Sunday school was ever seriously challenged. Now I was beginning my professional training in a school that I expected to be a bit more intense academically, but, in atmosphere, little different from what I had experienced in church youth groups, a peaceful and loving community of dedicated young men being prepared by equally dedicated and wise teachers for a life of service to Christ's Church. Hardly a month had passed before I realized that I had stepped into a war zone. By mid-century the curriculum of Protestant theological education, even in the South, had begun to change, partly due, as I wrote in the last chapter, to the influence of the theological ferment that was taking place in postwar Europe, but also, perhaps surprisingly, due to the influence of the writings of Sigmund Freud. Along with new approaches to biblical studies, a whole new discipline of pastoral psychology had been introduced. It was the latter that was particularly disturbing to the most conservative elements among the faculty and student body of the seminary. Those who embraced the idea that ministers might do well to call upon the insights of psychology and psychiatry in approaching their role as pastoral caregivers found themselves in constant conflict with biblical fundamentalists who rejected wholeheartedly the notion that what they saw as spiritual problems could be helped by anything other than prayer and Bible reading. And the conflict was open and intense. The battle lines were drawn and there was little meeting of the minds in the no-man's-land that separated the two camps. I don't believe that I have ever been in any situation for so long a time where the atmosphere was so charged with anger and hostility. Not exactly what I had expected in an institution dedicated to preparing young men to be the conduits of Christian compassion.

If I learned anything about religious fundamentalism from my four years in that environment, it was that it is not basically (fundamentally?) a religious phenomenon. It is not religious conviction or the inspiration of spiritual insight that leads one to embrace the notion that there is one final, absolute answer for life's perplexities and that there is only one way to know that answer. Fundamentalism is a carry over into religion of a universally felt human need for a personal sense of well-being in an alarmingly unpredictable world. We humans do not naturally opt for uncertainty and open-endedness; we are normally uncomfortable with loose ends. Not having a sense of what's going on around us or where we are heading can make us very anxious. The fear of being lost and abandoned is ingrained in us from earliest childhood, and the feeling of being adrift in a confusing universe, with our own mortality the only sure thing, can be critically unnerving. It should therefore be no surprise that we should be susceptible to offers of safe havens in the midst of the hurricanes of change, the promises of solid ground when the earth seems to be quaking around us, and assurances of simple, absolute solutions to life's mysteries. And that is precisely what religious fundamentalism purports to do. It offers certainty to the uncertain, safety to the anxious, reassurance to the doubtful, and an unchanging set of principles with which to confront a seemingly capricious and erratic world. And at first glance that sounds pretty appealing, if it works. The problem is that the fundamentalist formula turns out to be a prescription for a spiritual tranquilizer with some serious and dangerous side effects.

In the first place, fundamentalism is a spiritual growth inhibitor. As soon as individuals are seduced into accepting the notion that there is one true answer to the dilemmas that confound us, they obviously don't need to search any further. They don't need to question or change or bother themselves any longer with the perplexing problems with which we struggle precisely because we are human in a puzzling world. They've got it made, they have arrived, which sounds an awful lot like being dead to me. In the second place, the fundamentalist prescription introduces a feeling of "us against them," a sort of fortress mentality against the rest of the world. If I have the truth and you don't, then your failure or refusal to see the truth that I see, or your embrace of a position that in effect denies the truth that I cling to, makes you inherently dangerous to me. My one truth makes it necessary for me to either change you, or merely tolerate you as one who is hopelessly lost, or, in the extreme, reject you or even destroy you. My one truth will not allow me to engage you as a brother, or tolerate your views as acceptably different from mine, or, God forbid, learn from you. And because my need to cling to my belief in my one truth grows out of my deep anxieties and fears for my safety in a threatening world, when I see that world changing in ways that seem to undermine principles and values that I have held dear, I may get even more desperate and even more dangerous as I fight to hold on to my one pillar of certainty. Finally, religious fundamentalism is a dangerous addiction because it is based on an illusion, the illusion that there is a final answer available to us fallible and limited humans that will exempt us from the doubts and anxieties that come with the territory of self-conscious mortality. Those doubts and anxieties are part and parcel of the ambiguity into which we humans were born at the hinging moment of our evolution into full humanity (more about that later). There may be ways by which to ameliorate the effects of those basic fears and uncertainties, to keep us from losing hope and turning on one another, and that is one of our basic human tasks. But nothing will free us from the struggle to learn to live with them. There are no simple answers, no final truths, no perfect formulas, no instruction books, no embraceable dogmas, no get-out-of humanity-free cards that will grant us immunity from our responsibility to search out the meaning of our own lives.

There is certainly nothing about the Bible that inherently lends *it* to the use that religious fundamentalists make of it as the infallible handwriting of God, whose every word must be literally accepted as sacred truth. The Bible is a wide-ranging collection of many kinds of literature. It is more a library than a single book. It contains the myths and legends of an ancient people brought down through the ages from early oral tradition, the history of a relatively insignificant Middle Eastern tribe and their religious evolution, their wisdom and their poetry. It contains strangely surrealistic writings hardly decipherable to us today, the preaching of self-appointed prophets, the later accounts of the life and teachings of Jesus, and some of the letters of his early followers. The Bible is not a unified whole, but an aggregate of many traditions, writers, and fragmentary sources that was patched together over many centuries. We know, for instance, from careful textual examination of the four "Gospels" in their original languages that they were not written in their entirety by the four men whose name their titles bear, but are a pastiche of varied documents by a number of unknown sources that were brought together probably some time in the first hundred years after the death of Jesus. As we saw earlier, in the case of the official "canon" of the New Testament, the reasons for the inclusion of certain writings and not others were often based more upon institutional and political concerns than anything else. As recently as the sixteenth century there was a dispute over the inclusion of the book of Revelation in the list of New Testament books (and given the bizarre and troublemaking interpretations of this impenetrably mysterious piece of writing that have been put forward over the years, it probably would have been just as well if it had been left out). Catholics and Protestants have always disagreed on the inclusion of the inter-testamental books of the Apocrypha. Recently discovered "lost gospels," books on the life and teachings of Jesus written by some of his immediate followers, which were suppressed by the early Church fathers in an effort to consolidate their own power, have raised questions in many minds about the sanctity of the canon of "holy" scripture.

In some of the biblical writings, profound insights into the human situation and deep and abiding truths can be found, but it also contains much that has little or nothing of value to say to modern people (dietary rules governing what nomadic people can safely eat while wandering in the desert may be interesting from an historical standpoint, but that's about it, and the religious and moral notions of a culture only recently evolved out of the Stone Age can have little relevance for how we should regulate life in the twenty-first century). In any case the Bible is an assemblage of very human writings whose real integrity and value as such has been most compromised and corrupted by those who would make of it what it is not and was never intended to be, the divinely infallible rule of faith and life. One of the saddest ironies with respect to the Bible and its place in Western culture is that the worst distortions of its most profound truths (as we shall look at in a coming chapter) have been perpetrated by those who claim to honor it most. And the notion that scientific findings about the origins of the universe and the development of human life on earth are somehow in conflict with the great creation poem of the first chapter of Genesis is about as silly as suggesting that the six o'clock weatherman, with his meteorological descriptions of weather conditions, is attempting to deny the truth of Carl Sandburg's poem about fog.

It is past time to acknowledge openly, boldly and with no apologies to anyone, that a book is sacred because it is true; it is not true because it is considered by some to be sacred. There are no "holy books." All books are human in origin. Some may be more "inspired" than others, some may contain more truth than others, but all are human. To the extent that a book hits upon the truth—any book, whether it be a scientific treatise, a piece of fiction, history, poetry, philosophy, drama— that book is "sacred." All truth is sacred, whoever states it or in whatever form it is found. There is no "imprimatur" that can be placed upon a book in advance of the reader's consideration of it for himself that can guarantee its safety for the believer, its truth. The reader is never exempt from the responsibility of deciding for himself whether what he is reading strikes him as the truth or not. As it turns out Sportin' Life was right: "the things that you're liable to read in the Bible…ain't *necessarily* so" just because the word Holy is stamped in gold on the cover. The reader must decide. The truth is where you find it.

Some will protest, "But isn't that the road to chaos? If everyone is just free to decide for him or herself what is true and what is not, where will that lead us? Surely there has to be some authority to guide us in deciding what is right and what is wrong; we can't just have every individual believing whatever he wants to." But what are we really afraid of?

Is it the *freedom* to decide for oneself what one believes that frightens us, or is it, rather, the *responsibility* for making up our own minds that is so scary? Why do we trust ourselves so little that, rather than taking seriously our task of forging out for ourselves the meaning of our lives, we would turn them over to some outside authority? I am not suggesting that we are simply left to wander around in the dark, making up our lives as we go, as if no one had ever been down this path before. There is a great wealth of wisdom out there to call upon from others who have lived before us. But whatever light we opt to follow, the decision is still ours to make, and no one can take away from us the responsibility of making it wisely.

So, if you asked me what *I* know of the truth, how would I respond? I've asked myself that question many times. I certainly *know*—as we all do—a lot of stuff. I have a lot of information in my head about a lot of things. I know, for instance, a good bit about birds and other things in the natural world. I know how many primary and secondary feathers are in the wings of most birds and how they fit together and why birds' beaks are shaped the way they are. I know how to identify several hundred species of them by their size, shape, and coloration and a good many of them by the sound of their singing. I know the Latin names of some of the orders of insects and that *Coleoptera*, the order of hard-shelled beetles, contains more distinct living species than any other category of animated life on earth. Of trees and flowers, snakes and lizards, frogs and turtles, fish and mammals, I know perhaps a bit more than the average person and a whole lot less than an expert. I am acquainted with some of the stars in their constellations and know something about the planets of our solar neighborhood and how far a journey it is to the moon.

I know how airplanes fly and the names of just about every combat plane that fought for the United States, Britain, and Germany in World War II, and some that fought for Japan and the Soviet Union. I know that in World War I, Eddie Rickenbacker, the great American ace, flew a French-made Spad for the Lafayette Escadrille and that Germany's great ace, Baron von Richthofen, flew a bright red Fokker D-I. I've built models of them both. I know something of how an automobile engine functions, but not enough to work on one. I can do basic repairs on a flush toilet and can wire a simple electrical switch. I have done simple carpentry and sailed a small boat and I know how to score a tennis match. I know how to make an etching from a metal plate, a lithograph from a stone, and a multicolor serigraph from stencils mounted on stretched silk. With a pencil I can draw a picture of just about anything I can see, and I know how to cut a double mat in which to frame it.

I have surveyed art history and know the names of the major movements and can recognize the work of most of the leading painters, sculptors, and architects of their respective periods (though sometimes I forget their foreign-sounding names). I have written a thesis on the sixteenth century Protestant reformer John Calvin's reaction to the art of the Renaissance. I have seen enough classical ballet to know a good pirouette *en pointe* when I see one, and have listened to enough classical music to have my favorite composers and performers, symphonies, and concertos. I have sung bass in a church choir, a college chorus, and a barbershop quartet. I have read many of the literary classics and have studied four languages other than my own (without learning to speak any of them). I've read some of the New Testament in Greek and more of the Old Testament in Hebrew. I hold an undergraduate degree in English, two graduate degrees in Theology, and one in Studio Art.

But, after all of that, what do *I* really *know* of the *Truth*?

I know the transforming power of love. I know what it means to be loved. I know what it means for another person to look at me and see me as I am, and still to say to me, "I love you." I know what it means to be known, to be found out, to be stripped of pretense and dissembling, to be caught naked in the spotlight of another person's unapologetic gaze, and to have that person not look away because of my embarrassment, but simply say, "I love you." I know the humbling experience of laying out all my treasures before the one I most desire to please, whose favor I wish most to gain, to point out to that person all the things I can do, the knowledge I possess, the material goods I am offering to share, my winsome personality, and my moral rectitude, and then to know that I have not succeeded in buying anything with all I have to trade, that love is free. And something in me protests, "No! No, I don't want it for *free*. I want to *deserve* it. I want you to love me because I am good and handsome and strong and talented and cultured and wise." But my beloved, who receives with appreciation every good gift that I have to offer, still keeps no balance sheet of debits and credits against which to measure my performance. She simply loves me. And that is the truth that I know. That it is possible for human beings to love and be loved like that is a truth that defines the very meaning of our existence. That is the truth that can save us from ourselves. That is the saving miracle that can rescue us from the moralistic burden of self-righteousness, the tedious nervous need to be constantly measuring others against our yardstick of moral and social acceptability to ensure that they deserve our respect and compassion. That is the transforming truth that lifts the sex act above sweaty, self-seeking lust to become the gift of oneself for the pleasure of one's lover. That is the truth that makes a friendship something more than *quid pro quo,* a mutually advantageous contractual agreement. That is the truth that raises parenthood above the genetically programmed impulse to propagate the species and makes a family what it was meant to be. That is the truth that can enable friendship and marriage and parenthood to be the fullest expressions of our humanity. I have been loved like that, and I know that to be the truth.

And I know what it is to be overcome with absolute, unadulterated Joy. I am not talking now about "happiness," that state of being, the pursuit of which is a right guaranteed by our constitution, but which too often eludes us and melts out of our hands in the very act of our grasping for it. I am talking about joy, which always comes as a surprise and which can never be "attained" by the application of any strategy we may employ. Joy is not to be had; it can only be experienced. Joy cannot be predicted under any particular set of circumstances, but we can learn to expect it. Joy cannot be made to occur, but one can be open to its advent. Joy is what Wordsworth was describing when he wrote,

> *"My heart leaps up when I behold*
> *A rainbow in the sky:*
> *So was it when my life began;*
> *So is it now I am a man…"[2]*

Have we not all experienced those moments when our hearts leap with utter elation at some unexpected sight, at some unanticipated beauty, at the sudden appearance of some long-absent friend or lover? I have walked through green woods along the shore of a lake, when suddenly I glimpsed through the trees at the edge of the water the unexpected sight of a male hooded merganser in all the glory of his courting plumage and felt my heart leap with joy. I was sailing my small boat once just beyond the surf at Pawley's Island, South Carolina, when four porpoises, each longer than my tiny hull, surfaced to give me company for a few moments on my way, one on either side, one behind, and one in front as if to be my guides. I looked into their eyes, heard them blow out their breath, and felt my heart leap for joy. I came home years ago from a month's absence and got out of the car to see my five-year-old son charging at me from across the street where he had been playing, his arms wide, his legs pumping in total abandon, calling, "Daddy! Daddy!" at the top of his voice, and my heart leapt in harmony with his joy at seeing me. I have seen my wife, my beloved, turn a corner and come suddenly into view and felt my heart leap with the sheer joy of seeing her smiling face even when she had been out of my presence for only a brief time. Like the poet, my heart, too, leaps at the appearance of a rainbow, or the billowing of a building cumulus cloud in the rose light of the setting sun, or when a buckeye butterfly lands on my arm and begins to probe the pores of my skin with his coiled tongue to determine if I am of any use to him.

I do not know whether any members of the animal kingdom other than humans have the capacity for feeling and expressing joy, but I wonder about that when I hear the mockingbird singing from the top of his tree in front of our house, his music seeming altogether too complicatedly baroque for the mere purpose of declaring his territorial claims. He sounds awfully much like someone singing for the sheer pleasure of it. I recall once watching a pair of adolescent white-tailed deer who had been quietly feeding in a woodland glade under the nervous eye of the mother doe suddenly break loose into a game of chase. Around and around they went in gamboling abandon, seeming to fly between the trees and over dead wood, splashing through a rocky creek bed, never once losing their footing or breaking stride on their twiggy legs. They raced each other in a ragged circle around their mother who went on feeding, looking up occasionally to check for danger, patiently waiting, like many an indulgent mom, for her offspring to get the craziness out of their systems. And as I watched their delirious romp, I almost imagined I could hear their laughter giggling through the trees. Perhaps that is just another anthropomorphic projection of human feeling on to an animal world of purely instinctual behavior. But I am not so sure of that. What I *am* sure of is that for us humans, joy is a saving grace. Joy is what happens when we are suddenly grabbed out of ourselves—by the way sunlight touches a certain flower, by the sudden appearance around a corner of one's beloved, by the majesty of a blooming thunderhead, the smiling response of an infant child, the near approach of a curious hummingbird (the detonators of joyous explosions are infinitely unpredictable)—and we are rescued from our regular reticence and our guardedness, to fall, if only for the briefest moment, hopelessly in love with life. In the instant when we are captured and dragged out of ourselves by joy, we experience total freedom. But joy is too fleeting an experience to be clasped to one's breast or pocketed for later; it is too unpredictable to be programmed; it is not a right that any constitution can guarantee. It is the extraordinary fleeting gift that the world awards us for being human. And while we cannot make it happen, we can expect it to. We can learn to open ourselves to the moment when life offers us the gift of spontaneity. Joy is the antidote for boredom and despair; it is the bright side of the often frightening precariousness of life. I have known joy and I know that to be true.

And I have known the elevating leverage of Beauty. You have probably heard someone talk of being "uplifted" by a particularly beautiful passage of music, and that is an almost literally perfect description of the effect of beauty on the human spirit. It elevates our humanity. I am always hoisted up when I listen to my favorite CD of Hilary Hahn's performance of Samuel Barber's *Concerto for Violin and Orchestra*. Once, when I was fifteen years old, I was literally drawn up out of the mucky mess of adolescence by the mere sight over a Florida river of the exquisite grace of a swallow-tailed kite. I have been startled into rising ecstasy by the surprising color combinations and outlandish shape of an Indian pink wildflower pushing its way up out of the decayed-leaf floor of a Tennessee forest. I have been transported and removed from my seat by the singular elegance of the final *pas de deux* from *Swan Lake*. And the soaring melodies of Tchaikovsky's *Serenade For Strings* never fail to raise me out of the everydayness of my existence. Beauty does that. Beauty, in whatever form it appears to us, whether through art or nature, acts like a spiritual forklift hoisting us to higher levels of humanness. But beauty is *not* a luxury; it is as vital a food for the human spirit as bread is for the body. We simply cannot live humanly without it. Surely one of the most crippling effects of economic poverty is that it so often forces people to exist in habitats that are drab and ugly. People are "borne down" by poverty, and one of the heaviest weights bearing on them is the common drabness of their surroundings. Ugliness is a deadly poison to the human spirit. We must have beauty in our lives, or life will grind down to mere existence. I have known what it means to be lifted up by beauty, and I know that to be the truth.

And I have known the transcending impetus of Wonder. The capacity for wonder is perhaps the most uniquely human trait of all. It is the product of that exclusively human ability to stand outside ourselves and to know our own ignorance, to imagine what we do not know and worlds we cannot see or measure by our senses. That loving and contented pet dog or cat of yours does not know what he does not know; he cannot imagine any life other than the one that is immediate to him. Only we humans have the capacity, not only to benefit from what we know and understand, but to stand in awe of that which lies outside our ken. To be fully human, "a man's reach [must] exceed his grasp..." Not knowing is as important as knowing. All of that stuff I listed before, all that accumulation of information and knowledge that I have garnered over the years? That is the mere sediment that lies at the bottom of the river that flows from the wellspring of wonder. It is wonder that stands at the headwaters of all our knowledge. If technology is the engine that drives our thrusts of exploration out into the dark unknown, then wonder is its fuel.

A healthy diet of wonder is also what is needed to inoculate us against the deadly testosterone of pride, that uniquely human tendency to think of ourselves more highly than we have any right to think. We, as a species, are so greatly enamored with ourselves that we seem hardly to notice that there is precious life here other than our own. A little wonder-born humility would make us so much nicer to live with and would make it a whole lot easier for the non-human world to put up with us. We live in the world like a bunch of arrogant, self-indulgent, know-it-all adolescents who are too ignorant of the world outside the narrow confines of our own hormonal self-centeredness to think of anything but our own needs. In the universal schoolyard of life-in-the-world, we human children are failing in the plays-well-with-others category. If we don't grow up and stop prancing around the world as if we owned it, like *The Little Prince*[3] on his own little asteroid, we may well find ourselves facing expulsion from "planet school." I fear that we moderns have become so disconnected from our inclusive natural family that we are in danger of losing altogether that sense of awe and respect for life that can save us from our hubristic recklessness. The poet, William Wordsworth, says it again,

> *"This Sea that bares her bosom to the moon;*
> *The winds that will be howling at all hours…*
> *For this, for every thing, we are out of tune;*
> *It moves us not."*[4]

What will it take for us to get in tune with the world, to once again be so "moved" by the richness and variety of life around us that we will begin to care for its welfare as much as we lust after our own immediate comfort? It will, I believe, take nothing less than a rebirth of wonder.

I have knelt in the grass of a spring day to examine up close a flower so small that I almost missed noticing it from my eye-level altitude of about five feet, and I have discovered an object of such formal complexity and stunning beauty that I was silenced in mouth-gaping awe at the very existence of such a wondrous thing. Why should such glory as this be hiding out in this miniaturized reclusiveness? What is Mother

Nature's point in keeping this miraculous expression of hers a secret from us? I simply could not fathom it. And should you wish to know what sheer, mind-boggling wonder can do for you, it is this kind of experience that I recommend. No need to travel to the Grand Canyon or half a world away to some lush tropical isle or snowcapped mountain range. Just go outside in the spring and lie down next to the smallest flower you can find tucked away amidst the leaves of grass and look at it long enough and hard enough for its beauty to grab you. Ask of it what possible reason there could be for its existence. You might just hear it answer with a question about your own. Be warned, however; wonderment like that can change your life. I have experienced the transforming impetus of wonder and know that to be the truth.

Thumbtacked to the side of the bookshelf nearest my writing desk is a 3x5 index card on which I have copied a line I came across some time ago in Joseph Campbell's classic work, *The Power of Myth*.[5] It reads, "The experience of eternity right here and now is the function of life."[16] I have thought long and hard about that statement and asked myself over and over just what he meant by "experiencing eternity" in the here and now. Eternity, despite its common use, is a word that only superficially describes a *quantity* of time or length of life; it really has to do with certain *qualities* of life that transcend the temporal and the physical. So, what was Campbell talking about? What are the transcendent qualities that we can experience in the very midst of our daily lives? What words describe that "eternity"? I made lists of all the words I could think of that might encompass both the transcendence and the everydayness of which he wrote. My list started out long, got edited by much questioning of each term, and finally was distilled into just four words, four qualities, the four that I have been attempting to describe in the previous several paragraphs: Love, Joy, Beauty, and Wonder. You may come up with your own list of "eternal qualities"; don't accept my list without questioning your own experience. But these four seem to sum it up for me. And is Campbell right? Is this what it all comes down to? Can the very function and purpose of our existence be described as the living out in our daily lives of such transcendent qualities as love and joy and beauty and wonder? Could all of our puzzling about life's "mysteries" and "human destiny" and such profundities as those really come down to something so simple (and yet so complicated) as this? You will have to decide that for yourself, of course, but I have the feeling that he may just be on to something.

If there is such a thing as a "final answer" or an "ultimate truth" about the meaning of our existence on this earth, I am convinced that we will not find it contained in any creed or in the teachings of any particular religion or in the pages of any "sacred" scripture. All of those resources, however inspired they may have been originally, are still only human cultural expressions, conditioned by the historical experience of those who made them, frozen in time in the moment that they were formalized and written down. Surely the transcendence that we seek will not be limited by any such man-made boxes, however respected and venerated the containers may be. As an illustration of the point, I offer the following "parable" (actually, a true story). I know a man, whom I am privileged a call a personal friend, who, besides the surpassing musical talent for which he is widely known, has managed to combine an unbridled intellectual curiosity, a quirky sense of humor, a slightly skewed way of looking at the world with such an audacious and adventurous spirit that among those who know him best the stories of his most outlandish escapades have reached almost mythical proportions. My favorite example is the story (parable?) of the hurricanes and the mason jars. At one point in his young adult life, my friend became fascinated with hurricanes. He had grown up in a coastal, Southern state and had no doubt seen and felt the peripheral effects of those fierce tropical storms. But that was not enough for him. He longed to experience their awesome power personally and directly, and he came up with a bold and ingenious plan both for having and recording the experience. On several occasions when one of those cutely named menaces was bearing down on a particular section of the coast, he would get in his car and drive to the place where it was scheduled to come ashore, timing his arrival to coincide with the crossing inland of the eye of the storm. Each time, he took a case of pint-sized mason jars with him, the kind with the two-part sealable lids that are used for canning and preserving vegetables and jellies and jams. Finding some temporary shelter, he would wait out the lashing fury of the storm's outer wall until it passed and the calmness of the eye was upon him. Then he would take out his case of mason jars, open each of them to the outside air, and then, after a few minutes, he would reseal them and put them back in their pasteboard carton. Later each of them would be labeled, "Air from the Eye of Hurricane 'So-and-so,'" with the date and location of the storm's landfall, and they would be given as gifts to his friends, mementos of the storm.

I am sorry that I did not know him back then and so never received the gift of one of his wonderful jars of air. I would have cherished it. Not as the memento of a storm, but rather, as an endearing symbolic reminder of the man himself. The hurricane, with all its wind and rain and awesome power, was not in the jar. The mason jar, with its wonderfully absurd label, was not really about the storm itself; it was about the man who went to meet it and experience its majesty. The creeds, the doctrines, the teachings, the "holy" books are the mason jars that contain the stories of man's search for the ultimate truth about the mystery of his existence, and they are valuable as such. But they are not the truth itself. That truth will not be contained in any jar or in any box with a gilded lid. The truth lies in the "storm" itself. Jesus said, "The Kingdom of God is within you," and another teacher, Joseph Campbell, said, " The experience of eternity in the here and now is the function of life." I think they were talking about the same thing. I think they were talking about the capacity of each of us to experience the storm itself, not just to breathe the air from someone else's jar.

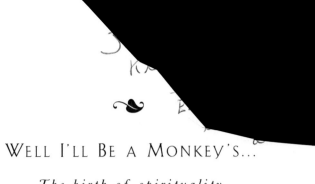

WELL I'LL BE A MONKEY'S...

The birth of spirituality

I HAVE NEVER BEEN MY AGE. I have never been contemporary with my contemporaries. From my earliest recollection I seem always to have been both older and younger than my peers, my classmates, and my playmates, older quite often in years and always years younger in appearance and physique. It was a problem that I came by naturally. My maternal grandfather, a dapper little man, never weighed more than one hundred and ten pounds in his life, and my mother was so petite that once in her middle years, when her weight reached nearly one hundred pounds, she felt an uncomfortable need to reduce (and she wasn't anorexic!). As a little boy I was so tiny that some of my neighborhood playmates nicknamed me "midget." And in the graduation photograph of my eighth grade class I am in the first row, shorter than the smallest girls, looking for all the world like an uncomfortable nine- or ten-year- old, embarrassed at having stumbled into the wrong picture. In only three months from the time of that photo I would be entering high school! While I was an active child, I wasn't especially athletic, being much too small to compete against boys my own age. I could certainly hold my own in the classroom, but on the playing field I

course, my social maturation was
size and childish appearance. All the
bigger than I was. My few early attempts
dancing were subverted by the embarrassment at
having to reach up over my head to put my hands where
they were supposed to be while trying to get my feet to move
in proper time to the music and avoid staring straight into
the intriguing valley between my partner's budding breasts.
I didn't get up the courage to ask a girl out until the middle
of my junior year in high school (when I took a girl named
Joann by city bus to a Boy Scout banquet), and I didn't have
a real girlfriend until I was in college.

All in all, mine was an awkwardly stressful early adolescence. In high school I was just plain out of it, too immature
sexually and socially to participate in the hormonally charged
teenage ritual of courtship and dating. With no group membership in school to give me a sense of belonging, I was just
a lonely little boy going through the motions of class work,
painfully putting up with the teasing I took because of my
name, constantly afraid of the bullies who terrorized my beloved woodworking class by routinely vandalizing the tools
and threatening to destroy the work of anyone who dared to
report them. I was a miserable misfit, and for the whole first
year of high school I dreaded returning to those alien halls.
That would change, but only very slowly. But something else
was about to happen that would abruptly focus my life and
that would, in time, help to shape the course of my being in
the world. The new focus was what I saw through the lenses
of a pair of bird-watching binoculars.

96

My family had relocated from South Carolina to Birmingham, Alabama, in the first spring of World War II and had moved into a second floor apartment in an older building in the area of the city known as the South Highlands. On the other side of town, the steel mills and iron foundries of that "Pittsburgh of the South" were busily belching the smoky refuse of wartime production into the ever leaden skies over the city. At night the western horizon seemed to blaze with the fires of hell from the glow of the Bessemer converters refracted by the particulates in the polluted air. And everything got dirtier in that place than anywhere I have ever been. Our clothes got dirtier; the curtains and window ledges in the apartment were always sooty; our small, screened porch was too dirty for me to play on. Even the trees and shrubs collected the coal dust fallout from the mills. When I came in from playing in the overgrown vacant lot across the street I would have black around my nostrils, in the corners of my eyes, and in my ears. I wonder now how my mother, the "High Priestess of Clean," ever survived those sooty war years with no washing machine, no shower, no place to hang clean clothes to dry. Over the years, I have come to think of her affectionately as one who, though she staunchly professed her belief in God, was one who, in practice, actually believed in Soap. Cleanliness was not just next to godliness, it was the same thing. She must surely have dreamed of living again some day in a place where the air was clean and she had at least a fighting chance in her lifelong struggle against dirt. Those dreams came true

97

in the summer of 1947 when my father was able to place a down payment on a small bungalow in the southern suburb of Homewood, across the dividing barrier of Red Mountain from the filth and pollution of the city. It was only a small house, with not much more space than the apartment where we had spent the last five years, but it was clean, it had a yard and a nice front porch, and, best of all for me, it backed up to a small woodland of pine and hardwood, thick with undergrowth and teeming with birds. Almost from the day we moved in, I was hooked.

I don't know what it was about birds that grabbed my interest. Some might conclude that my sudden obsession was merely a compensation for the dreariness of my school and social life, and there may be some truth in that. But whatever it was that called out to me from that woodland population of feathered variety that was suddenly spilling into my new backyard as into my awareness, I was snared, possessed, and redirected by the need to know about these lively and beautiful creatures. Birds suddenly became my world. I soon acquired my first field guide (Richard Pough's *Audubon Bird Guide: Eastern Land Birds*, illustrated by Don Eckelberry[1]), and shortly thereafter my first binoculars (a pair of 7x50s, "made in occupied Japan"). I recall with almost total clarity the first bird I ever identified using my new field guide and new binoculars: it was a rufous-sided towhee. Though I had already been able to identify some of the most common birds, that towhee will always stand as the number one bird on my "life list." Oh, yes, I did become, and remain to this day, a keeper of lists.

Soon I was spending almost all of my spare time learning to identify the birds that populated "my woods," and it wasn't long before I discovered other places within pedaling distance from my house on my old Schwinn bike that attracted a different variety of species from those found in what was, to me, my own private bird sanctuary. My "life list" began to grow, and along with it grew my confidence. I was a changed person. I had found the consuming passion that liberated me from my uncertainties about myself. When school began next term, I went back without the dread that I had experienced in my first year, and even though it felt so much easier to be there, I still couldn't wait for the school day to end, but now I couldn't wait because my binoculars and my birds were waiting for me. Almost every day when I got home from school, as soon as I could throw down my books and change my clothes, I was out the back door and headed for the woods. During that fall, I became the youngest member of the Birmingham Audubon Society. I was welcomed into the club by as kind and gentle a group of men and women as I have ever known, most of whom were as old, or older than, my parents. I never missed a meeting (held at the Birmingham Public Library, about a forty-five minute trip for me by city bus), and went on all of the club's organized field trips. I soon became something of a "young star" of the Audubon Club, not because of my expertise as a birder, but because of my enthusiasm and eagerness to learn. Each December we participated in the annual Christmas Bird Count sponsored by the National Audubon Society. In 1948 I had one of the great thrills of my young life when I was asked to make up half of a two-man team for the Christmas Count with Tom Imhof, the *real* star of the group. The best birder I have ever known personally, Thomas A. Imhof would later write the definitive book on the birds of Alabama.[2]

At the same time, I began to paint birds. I had been drawing since I was old enough to hold a pencil, a skill I picked up following my big brother's example. As youngsters we spent countless hours filling up reams and reams of "office paper," which our father would bring home from his workplace, with drawings, mostly of the airplanes and automobiles that claimed our boys' imaginations. It seems only natural that I would turn that facility with a pencil to the expression of my newfound passion for birds. But because birds are all about color, I wanted to paint them. So, I purchased a set of watercolors and got to work. Now I was filling up stacks of cheap watercolor paper with paintings of birds, using as my "models" the illustrations in my growing collection of bird books. I know now that that was a mistake. My bird paintings remained stiff and lifeless because I had foregone the basic discipline of learning to draw them from life. But I struggled on, if not very skillfully, as least enthusiastically, filling up lots of paper with little that promised any kind of future as a successful bird artist. It would be many years later, after my "detour" into the ministry, after a graduate degree in studio art, after I had honed my pencil powers of observation, after several years of teaching printmaking and developing my own techniques as an etcher, that I would return to that first subject of my personal art and begin to turn out the etchings that have given me some right to be known as a "bird artist."

In the almost sixty years that have passed since the day I first experienced that singular thrill of discovery, when my field guide and binoculars told me that the lively little black and white and rufous bird scratching at the leaves in my new backyard was a towhee, my love affair with birds has never gone away. It has cooled at times when other temporarily more compelling needs claimed my attention. But even when they were "out of sight," the birds have never been far "out of mind." They have always waited like a long-suffering lover for my return to claim them and their special place in my life. And after a lifetime of lists...after a lifetime of tromping through woods, wading through creeks, lying next to ponds with elbows mushed into mud, struggling with ice-covered binoculars while scanning some freezing lake for winter ducks, trudging for hours through loose coastal sands in 100-degree heat, all in search of the elusive "lifer"...after the numberless hours of waiting in still silence for the objects of my gentle pursuit to show themselves...after hundreds and hundreds of portraits of my avian loves—paintings, sketches, drawings, and etchings...after sharing my excitement with others who loved it like I did and suffering the humoring smiles of those who just didn't get it...what have I gained from all of this effort? I mean, of course, besides my early salvation from a miserable adolescence, almost six decades of joy, excitement, adventure and intellectual stimulation, many good friends, the chance to turn other people on to birding, a reason to travel to new and exciting places, and a satisfying career as a bird artist? If all of that were not enough, what has it meant to me in a deeper sense—do I dare to use the pretentious word—philosophically?

I think two things. First, what saved my life early on and has since provided me with a haven against the crackling madness of the world is that I learned how to be alone. I learned how to be alone and not be lonely. I learned how to be quiet. I learned out there in the woods with nothing to keep me company but the birds, the richness, the pleasure, and the practice of solitude. I learned that, no matter how important the outside stimulation of relationships with family and friends, social activities, entertainment, and intellectual and cultural input may be, all of that must be balanced for me by uninterrupted periods of deep and quiet aloneness, times for simply listening to the sound of my own breathing, times for listening to the silent music of my personal response to the universe. And as I grow older and find myself looking forward to my next big "career move," that of getting out of the world with as much grace as possible, those times of solitude and quiet reflection, which I found originally with the birds, become even more important.

The second thing that I learned watching birds is that they are part of my family, and I mean that both figuratively and quite literally. My lifelong intimate involvement with the natural world through the study of birds has convinced me that I am part of the natural world, and that is not a figure of speech. It is not some fuzzy, romantic notion from a starry eyed, bird-brained nature lover. It is a hard-nosed genetic reality. For me to imagine that I am some sort of special creature who, as a human being, stands over against the natural world with the non-consequential authority and power to use it for my own purposes is not only to be guilty of the most radical arrogance, it is to live by a colossal and ultimately life-and-earth-threatening falsehood. We *Homo sapiens* are, without doubt, a unique species, but that singularity is a matter of our being the highest evolved among our kin, and unless we understand both the nature of our uniqueness and the depth of our connection with our natural family, we will fail to reach our capabilities both as spiritual beings and as responsible inhabitants of the planet. And both of those failures are fraught with serious consequences.

One of the dubious distinctions that belongs to a citizen of the state of Tennessee—as I have enjoyed being for over forty years—is that one gets to share in the inheritance of one of the most famous—or infamous—events in American history, the Scopes Monkey Trial, which took place in 1925 and put the sleepy little town of Dayton, Tennessee, (population approximately 1,800 at the time) on the national map.[3] Most, but not all, Tennesseans today are probably somewhat embarrassed to own up to the international ridicule that was brought upon our state by its leadership role in the anti-evolution movement of the early twentieth century, which resulted in the whole South being seen by the rest of the world as intellectually and educationally retarded. The trial itself is almost lost to view by all the dust that was raised in Dayton by the full-blown media circus it became and by the mythologizing of the event that has occurred over the last eighty years.

The Scopes trial took place right in the middle of the "Roaring Twenties," and it was as much an expression of its times as the flapper, the raccoon coat, and the Charleston.

It was an uproarious time and it was a time of big changes in the United States. The Great War was over and the "doughboys" had come home from France, having helped to give America a new place on the world scene. One popular song that ushered in the decade asked the question, "How you gonna keep 'em down on the farm, after they've seen Paree?" The country was confident and prosperous and it seemed as if everyone was having fun. Life was speeding up. The first commercial radio stations went on the air in 1920, the automobile was displacing the horse and buggy, and barnstorming pilots trained to fly in the war were introducing aviation to the country's small towns and pastures.

It was also a time of reaction. There was a lot going on in this exciting new age to make previously isolated Americans nervous. Immediately following World War I, a new threat to capitalist democracy had been introduced onto the world stage in the form of international communism. There was much unrest among the usually docile labor force. And for the first time, modern science was being perceived as a real threat to the religious underpinnings of American society. Darwin's *The Origin of Species* had been published in 1859, and twelve years later there appeared his even more controversial *Descent of Man*, in which he spelled out his belief that humans and the great apes belonged to the same family. While the storm of controversy over these two books was intense, resistance to Darwinism in this country did not get well organized until after the war when his theories began to show up in science textbooks and news circulated of fossil finds, which were widely proclaimed to prove that evolution was a fact. The hunt for the "missing link" became a preoccupation of scientists and laymen alike. It was during this time that, not incidentally, the fundamentalist movement was catching fire in the more conservative Christian churches across the country. Opposition to the teaching of evolution became a rallying cry for those who believed that the Bible must be interpreted literally as the infallible word of God and that any teaching that differed from the Genesis version of creation was the work of the Devil. Several state legislatures across the country, bending to the pressure of fundamentalist Christians, entertained the idea of outlawing the teaching of evolution in the public schools. Tennessee was the first state to actually enact an anti-evolution statute.

There was, perhaps surprisingly, a lot of resistance in the state to the passage of such a law. It came in the form of newspaper editorials, public statements from university professors, the counsel of moderate clergy, and a few of the more liberal legislators. Even the governor, Austin Peay, was fairly lukewarm about signing the bill, but political considerations and his own religious convictions, along with his apparent naive belief that not much would come of it, prevailed over his usually progressive instincts and he signed it into law. Not much indeed might have come of it had not the newly formed American Civil Liberties Union at just that moment been looking for ways to promote its program for individual rights and academic freedoms. Tennessee's new anti-evolution law seemed made to order, and on May 4, 1925, an ACLU press release appeared in the *Chattanooga Times*, which had opposed the legislation, offering to challenge the law: "We are looking for a Tennessee teacher who is willing to accept our services in testing this law in the courts." The first shot in the ensuing battle had been fired, but the ACLU's offer fell on deaf ears in Chattanooga. No Chattanooga teacher stepped forward to pick up the gauntlet. But in the languishing little town of Dayton, some thirty miles north of Chattanooga, the ACLU's appeal struck a responsive chord.

Dayton, which had not even appeared on a map of Tennessee until the late nineteenth century had apparently already seen its best days. Located on the banks of the Tennessee River between Knoxville and Chattanooga, the town had been founded over deposits of coal and iron. When a Northern mining company had built a blast furnace there to take advantage of its underground wealth, the town's population had risen to a peak of 3,000, but the venture had not proved economically sustainable. The blast furnace had closed and almost half the population had moved on. Now concerned civic leaders were looking for something that would stimulate outside interest in their town. To a group of businessmen gathered in the town drugstore the day after the ACLU's ad appeared in the newspaper, it seemed they had found just what they were looking for. In contrast to the way in which the situation would be portrayed in later rewrites -- particularly in the play and movie *Inherit the Wind*[4] (which merely used the Scopes trial as a metaphor for the dangers of McCarthyism)—the men who decided to bring John Scopes to trial were not crusading conservative Christians. Conservative Christians they probably were, but their motive was publicity, not the prosecution of dangerous liberal ideas. And Scopes was no martyr for the cause of academic freedom; he was a young part-time science instructor and high school football coach who had been substituting for the regular biology teacher when, in a routine, end-of-term review, he had read from the approved science textbook that mentioned evolution in passing. He hadn't been dragged from the classroom and accused of corrupting the young, as the play and movie depicted the situation. He was just a convenient subject who was willing to let himself be used in a public relations effort that his recruiters thought would be good for the town. Neither he nor anyone else thought any harm would come to him, and none did. What these drugstore strategists did not understand, however, was that they had just poked their exploratory stick into the hole of a hornet's nest.

The biggest hornet to come buzzing out was William Jennings Bryan. Bryan was one of the best-known public figures of his day. He was a great orator who had served briefly as the U.S. Secretary of State under Woodrow Wilson until he resigned in protest over Wilson's intention to take the country into World War I. Three times he had been an unsuccessful Democratic candidate for president. He was also a staunchly fundamentalist Christian and, in recent years, had become the self-appointed leader of the anti-evolution movement, crisscrossing the country preaching with the passion of a zealot against the evils of evolutionary teaching. Now he came with the offer to assist in the prosecution of John Scopes. If the civic leaders of Dayton had been looking for publicity, having a lightning rod like William Jennings Bryan in town seemed guaranteed to get them more than they bargained for. To further complicate matters for the ACLU, which had hoped for nothing more than a simple case on the merits of the law, Bryan's appearance in the lists as the "White Knight" of Christian righteousness, brought galloping on to the scene his staunchest opponent, the brilliant defense attorney, Clarence Darrow, who was almost as passionate about his agnosticism and his opposition to religious interference in public affairs as Bryan was about his Christian mission to root out evil in society. This was not going to be a trial in any ordinary sense of that word; it was turning into a public joust between two great champions of opposing philosophies.

As it turned out, the trial was pretty much a disappointment to everyone concerned. While it briefly put Dayton on the map of public attention, the crowds, which the town officials had expected, were smaller than anticipated and the hoped for economic benefits never materialized (the only things the town got out of it in the long run were a reputation for backwardness and the establishment of a fundamentalist Christian college named after William Jennings Bryan). Bryan never got the chance to show off his oratorical mastery. The only time he was able to speak at any length during the trial came when Darrow, through some crafty legal maneuvering, got him called to the stand as a witness for the defense and proceeded to humiliate him by his antagonistic interrogation. Then Darrow robbed him of the chance even to make a closing statement by unexpectedly conceding the prosecution's case and changing the defendant's plea to guilty. The trial ended with Scopes being convicted and fined one hundred dollars for breaking the state ordinance against teaching evolution. But nothing was really decided. The ACLU did not get a clear precedent it could build on. The fundamentalists could claim victory because of the verdict (which was later overturned by the Tennessee Supreme Court on a legal technicality), but the humiliation of their champion was a bitter pill (Bryan died less than a week after the trial ended). While there seemed to be a consensus in the country that the pro-evolutionists had won the debate, if not the trial, that, too, was inconclusive. As for John Scopes, who was never more than a minor player in the affair, he left Dayton immediately after the trial and slipped back into the obscurity from which he had briefly emerged. The Tennessee law against the teaching of evolution in the public schools remained on the books until its repeal in 1967, but it was never openly challenged again, nor seriously enforced.

Thus, the much heralded "Trial of the Century" (how many other judicial contests have been tagged with that bit of hyperbole?) resulted in a veritable stalemate. And since 1925, the debate over evolution between science and Christian fundamentalism has remained relatively dormant. Until recently. As in 1925, today, when the world is once more going through a period of drastic and unnerving change, religious fundamentalism has raised its anxious head and begun to look around for an enemy to attack. And the tired old debate is raging again. Today, when the argument is joined, it is heard more often in terms of "pro-creationism" or something called "intelligent design" (an attempt to refurbish and redirect one of the weary old philosophical "arguments for the existence of God" that were already considered to be merely intellectual exercises when I had to study them in theological seminary fifty years ago). The reactionary strategy, however, remains the same: conservative Christians insisting that their biblical version of the origins of human life be taught in the public schools, if not exclusively, at least as an alternative view alongside the scientific "theory" of evolution. The first problem with that is that evolution is not a mere theory as the evangelicals like to term it. In a recent issue of *National Geographic* magazine ("Was Darwin Wrong?" November, 2004), David Quammen defines a scientific theory:

> *Evolution by natural selection, the central concept of the life's work of Charles Darwin, is a theory. It's a theory about the origin of adaptation, complexity, and diversity among Earth's living creatures. If you are skeptical by nature, unfamiliar with the terminology of science, and unaware of the overwhelming evidence, you might even be tempted to say that it's "just" a theory. In the same sense, relativity as described by Albert Einstein is "just" a theory. The notion that Earth orbits around the sun rather than vice versa, offered by Copernicus in 1543, is a theory. Continental drift is a theory. The existence, structure, and dynamics of atoms? Atomic theory. Even electricity is a theoretical construct, involving electrons, which are tiny units of*

charged mass that no one has ever seen. Each of these is an explanation that has been confirmed to such a degree, by observation and experiment, that knowledge-able experts accept it as fact. That's what scientists mean when they talk about a theory: not a dreamy and unreliable speculation, but an explanatory statement that fits the evidence.[5]

It is simply a well-established, scientifically demonstrable *fact* that life on earth has evolved over millions of years from simple to complex organisms, from lower forms to higher. While there may be debates within the scientific community about *how* evolution has proceeded, there is virtually a total consensus regarding the basic facts. Darwinism may have been one man's hypothesis early on; today it is as much a fact as gravity or electricity.

The second problem with the creationists' strategy is that, in order to entertain a discussion with Christian fundamentalists over the question, one must grant—if only for the sake of discussion—the validity of their argument based on their interpretation of the Bible as a record of historical and scientific facts regarding the origins of the universe and its inhabitants. If one does not accept that interpretation, (and I certainly do not. I believe that creationism is as much an assault on the Bible as it is an attack on science; by turning the Bible into a book of "proof texts" for the undergirding of their faltering faith, the fundamentalists distort its purpose and violate its true nature), then there is no ground for a debate at all. There can be no meeting of the minds and no compromise. The only issue that remains is whether a strictly religious view—and a very narrow one at that—should be mandated as part of the public school curriculum. And I would have thought that that issue should have been settled long ago.

But the biggest problem stemming from the so-called war between science and religion regarding evolution is that it has distracted us from the real relevance of evolutionary teaching for the way we shape our spiritual/religious response to the world around us. We have been so preoccupied with the debate over "origins" that we have tended to miss what the knowledge of evolution teaches us about our place in the universe. Ian Tattersall, in his wise book *Becoming Human: Evolution and Human Uniquenes*, puts it quite succinctly: "Human beings are part of nature. We are the results of the same processes that have produced all of the other myriad life-forms in the world."[6] That is the important lesson that the evolutionary sciences have to teach us, that we are an integral part of the natural world and that we are not exempt from the laws that govern it. On first reading that might seem obvious, but we have not always acted as if we understood it. Tattersall goes on to discuss how our relationship to nature changed when our early ancestors transitioned from being "hunter-gatherers" to being "agriculturists." Based on recent studies of remaining primitive peoples, he suggests that as hunter-gatherers, though they were exploiting nature for their own uses, our early forebears never saw themselves as standing over nature as its conquerors; they didn't experience themselves as separate from the natural world. When they became farmers—a development that may have occurred in response to climate changes—they began not just to use nature, but to change it, to reshape it according to their own designs. "For," Tattersall writes, "an agriculturist life is not a matter of cleverly exploiting what nature has to offer; rather it becomes a battle with nature, a matter of sidestepping the environmental vicissitudes through the application of technology. The battle may be lost or won, but it is a battle, nevertheless, between two opposing forces."[7]

This change in attitude, which now has humans standing over nature rather than within nature, was given a huge stamp of approval and the impetus of divine blessing early in the Judeo-Christian tradition when God is heard to say in the Genesis poem of creation, "...be fruitful and multiply, and fill the earth and subdue it, and have dominion...over every living thing that moves upon the earth" (Gen. 1:28, RSV). We humans have liked the sound of that, because those words seem to represent our coronation as God's viceroys on earth, giving us permission to do with it whatever we will. As Tattersall puts it, we see ourselves as " ...the monarchs of the ecosystem in which we live; we have been given dominion over it by a higher power."[8] Perhaps another reason we have so resolutely resisted the idea of human evolution—apart from our distaste at thinking of ourselves as cousins to the apes—is that it calls into question our exalted position as "lords of the earth." There is no doubt that we do occupy a unique position in relation to the rest of nature, or that we have the capacity to lord it over the earth. But recently, our place upon that throne has not seemed as comfortable as it once did. Perhaps we are beginning to feel that, in the words of Shakespeare's Henry IV, "…uneasy lies the head that wears a crown."

We are beginning to realize that what we have achieved as a result of our "adversarial" relationship with the natural world has not been an unmixed blessing. We are forced to come to terms not only with our power over nature, but with the mistakes we have made in our management of that power. We are learning that the earth's resources are not inexhaustible. We cannot go on using up its natural wealth as if there were no tomorrow. We have gaily gone our way "being fruitful and multiplying and filling the earth," but now we are being brought up short by the warnings of scientists that there is a limit to the size of the human population that the earth can sustain. The estimates vary as to what the numbers are, as do projections regarding when we will reach that limit. But there *is* a limit and we *are* approaching it, and we have not as yet found the political will to do anything significantly to slow the population growth. We wonder what kind of disaster it will take to wake us up to that necessity (was the toll of destruction of life and property from the recent tsunami and gulf hurricanes due to the overpopulation of coastal areas?). There was a time when it was feasible for a local population, such as for instance, the inhabitants of Easter Island in the Pacific or the modern island nation of Haiti, to exhaust totally the resources of their isolated homelands and to die out or simply move on to another place without having much impact on the rest of us. That is no longer true. We have run out of places to escape to when we have messed up our own backyards. Nor

can we build a wall around our own local ecosystem. There
is one global ecosystem upon which we are all dependent.
We will all save it, or we will cease to exist as a viable species.
It is as simple as that. There are no parts of the animal
family—our family—independent of all the other parts, just
as there are no places on earth unaffected by the sickness or
health of the whole planet.

We are part of nature. Our human place is not outside
the natural world, but within it. If we are descended directly
from the great apes, then we are also cousins to every living
species, and as they are totally dependent upon the green
world and its bounty for life and health, then so are we.
That is what the evolutionary sciences have to teach us.
And what does this have to say to our sense of ourselves as
religious/spiritual beings? Two things, I think. The first is
that we must change the "marching orders" we imagined
we received from the Old Testament. Recently I came
across an astounding passage in a late nineteenth century
book on American birds. The author, a very knowledgeable
amateur ornithologist and a Protestant clergyman, writes in
his preface that one of his purposes in publishing this book
is to encourage his fellow pastors to take up the study of
birds, that they "may show to the people the thoughts of an
infinitely wise and good Creator embodied in the universe."
Then, at the end of a section devoted to his detailed and
admiring observations of a sparrow hawk (the bird we know
today as the American kestrel), he concludes, "...the flight
is within close range of a shotgun, and, much as this elegant
and useful little Falcon merits human protection, *I reflect that*

all things—even birds—are made for man, and so drawing the lock on him bring him down."[9] (italics mine) Where did this preacher get the idea that "all things—even birds—are made for man"? He certainly did not get it from his study of birds and what they teach us about the "infinitely wise and good Creator." He got it from the Old Testament's injunction giving man dominion over the earth. And as shockingly out of step with our contemporary environmental sensitivities as this man's arrogance appears, we can by no means claim that he represents an attitude that has been expurgated from our dealings with nature. We are still acting as if we were God's viceroys on earth. We are still acting as if the earth were given to us to use according to our own selfish designs. And that must change. We must declare, once and for all, that that Old Testament injunction is null and void, and openly acknowledge that our past obedience to that so-called divine commission has been a tragic error on the part of humans in general, and of Western civilization in particular. Obviously we cannot go back to a time when humans had an easy undifferentiated sense of their oneness with the natural world; we are several thousand years late for that. But perhaps it is not too late for a change of attitude on our part.

That is what is called for: not merely new strategies for protecting our planet, not endless arguments over drilling for oil in pristine wilderness areas, not more speculation and debate about whether or not global warming is a fact, not more arbitrary regulations concerning allowable levels of air-polluting automotive emissions, etc., etc.,

etc. What *is* called for is a whole new attitude toward the natural world and our place in it, or, rather, a whole new attitude based upon our undeniable place in it, an attitude shaped by a deep feeling for our place in nature. It is not enough simply to be educated regarding the facts of our environmental precariousness. Somehow we must find ways of reconnecting with the natural world. If we as individuals and as a society do not *feel* our kinship with nature we will go on rationalizing our destructive uses of its resources until it is too late to save it or ourselves. To that end, we must begin to aggressively pursue programs designed to "re-connect" our children to the natural world from which we have allowed them to become alienated. The environmental scientists are teaching us that the planet cannot sustain a population whose religion gives them permission to use the earth as if it were their plaything. The evolutionary scientists are showing us a way to change our relationship to our planet and all of its inhabitants by teaching us to respect our animal heritage, to *love ourselves as animals* and thus to love and respect our animal cousins as we would members of our own family. In so doing we may also learn to love the earth as our extended family's home place. There is hope in that.

But the story of evolution not only has much to teach us concerning our place in the natural world; it has much to tell us about those peculiar qualities that distinguish us from our animal cousins. As the subtitle of Ian Tattersall's book (*...Evolution and Human Uniqueness*) suggests, the special capacities that make humans unique in the animal world, the capacities to be scientists, artists, poets, writers, musicians, planners, and builders are the products of evolution. And if it is true that we humans are the only religious animals—then is it not also quite likely that our spiritual/religious natures are the products of evolution? Indeed, I believe that we will never fully understand ourselves as spiritual beings until we have acknowledged the truth of that and have begun to understand the significance of that truth. Nor will we really grasp what spirituality and religion are essentially about until we see them in the light of the story of human evolution. I am convinced that the persistence of religion as a continuing stream that runs through all of human history can be fully explained only by reference to what happened as our earliest ancestors evolved into full human life.

One of the books in my personal library that I especially cherish is a volume put together by a wonderfully obsessive and brilliant woman who, fortunately for me, happened to be a very distant cousin of mine.[10] I feel lucky that she belonged to the DuBose clan because of her passion for genealogy, which, after many years of painstaking detective work, resulted in a remarkably complete "tree" of family connections on my father's side all the way from the birth dates of my own two sons back to our French Huguenot forefather, Isaac Dubosc, who landed in Charleston in 1689 as a refugee from Louis XIV's Catholic armies. The *DuBose Genealogy* contains no anecdotal material, no family stories; it is simply a 530-page chain-link pattern of names that reaches back to one man's arrival in the raw wilderness of seventeenth-century South Carolina in search of religious freedom. On the front endpapers of the book there is a photocopy of a sketchy family tree, hand drawn and written in French, that further traces the Dubosc family back to 1300 in Normandy, but that is as far as it goes. Dorothy MacDowell, our family's intrepid researcher, apparently ran into the reality that must be the bane of every dedicated genealogist: she reached to the point at which the records ran out.

Therefore, should I wish to continue the journey back down that genetic pipeline in search of my origins, I will have to go on alone with only my imagination as a guide, for beyond the year 1300 there are no dates, no family names, no place names to connect me to my ancient ancestors. Yet I know that they are there. I cannot see their faces, I cannot know their names, and I have no map on which to chart their specific route to the future. But they are there, plodding along for thousands of years through the obscuring mists of unrecorded history, doggedly making their way up the long genealogical road toward me. I know also that if I will just stay the course and keep forging back down that shrouded path, I will eventually come out of total darkness into a fairly well lighted place and time. It is a place and time that is lit for me by the findings of evolutionary scientists. They have shown us that if we trace our ancestry back far enough we will arrive at point beyond which our genetic forebears were hominids more closely related to the large apes than to creatures we would recognize as *Homo sapiens*. If we will follow the clues left by the fossil record back down the hidden corridors of time, we will arrive eventually at a point of transition when ape became man. And I have traveled back in imagination to that early morning of my human family's awakening, and this is what I believe I see there.

I see my earliest ancestor standing in the hinging moment of human evolution. He seems troubled, or at least puzzled by something. Mind you, this turning of the "hinge" did not occur in a sudden "moment" of time; it was a process that likely took place over thousands of years, and most likely did not occur as an evenly paced process among that population of hominids who were turning *Homo sapien*. They were changing, and no doubt some felt the change happening before others were aware of it, and those early observers must have wondered about it. What was going on? Something very strange was taking place. For one thing, they had never before even thought to ask about what was "going on." They had never had these kinds of feelings or these kinds of questions. If they had had feelings, they simply acted on them; they didn't stop to wonder why they were doing what they were doing or think about how they felt about it. And to further complicate their new situation they began to see the future! What must that have been like when our first ancestors realized that they could imagine what would occur tomorrow and what might take place even in the distant future, even to the time of their own deaths. Death? They were going to die? None of their kin among the animals had ever thought about *that* before. They had certainly seen death. They had killed other animals and, yes they had seen members of their own group be killed or just die for some reason. But they had never thought about it, at least for very long, and they had certainly never been able to project themselves into the future to contemplate their own deaths. And, they discovered something else that was totally new: they could now project themselves into the thoughts and feelings of others like themselves. They could feel what others felt. They could care about others of their group in a way that they had never experienced before.

So they started asking questions. Who were they becoming? They weren't like the animals with whom they shared the forests and the prairies, even though they were obviously kin to them. They ate like animals, they defecated like animals, they had sex like animals, they sought shelter from the storms like animals, and they died like animals. But they were not just animals; they thought, they felt, they cared for each other, they dreamed about the future, they built ever more complicated structures and devised ever more efficient tools, they planned ahead, and they worried about dying. What did all of it mean, that they were still part of the familiar world, were totally dependent upon it and its resources, and yet were separate from it, aliens in their own home? At one and the same time they felt both alienated from and connected to all they saw around them and they needed to make sense of that contradiction. What is important to note here, I think, is that with the birth of *Homo sapiens* came not only the birth of the *future* as an idea to deal with, but also the birth of *meaning*. And with the birth of meaning came the birth of *spirituality*. It was not until our earliest ancestors had passed the turning of the evolutionary hinge, and stood up in their full humanity that the question, "What does it mean?" occurred to them.

121

That *is* the spiritual/religious question, is it not? What is the meaning of my life? Who am I? What am I doing here? What is my connection to all of this? What sense am I to make of my existence?

And what did they do about all of their questions? They did what humans have always done. They began to bring some order into their disturbingly disordered and tangled new experience of the world in order to make some kind of sense out of it all. They began to give shape to the confusion that they were feeling about their new status. They began to come up with possible answers to their questions, and *Homo religiosus* was born. I can imagine it happening something like this. Looking around them at their world they began to see patterns that repeated over and over again; there was an order to their world that they had not noticed before. They saw the regularity of the rising and setting of the sun and the changing of the seasons, and they must have noticed in the green world of trees and plants the cycles of death and rebirth that occurred in concert with the seasonal changes from the cold and dark of winter to the bright warmth of the summer when the sun returned with its life-giving power. Was the sun the first object of early man's worship, the first "ordering" notion that began to make some sense of his bewilderment at being human? Was this how that original, unfocussed spiritual quest gained shape and content, from this "bright idea" that the sun might just be the ultimate source from which all of life derives its existence? It might well have been for some tribes of early people. For some others it might have been the mystery of the beginning of life as witnessed in the miracle of birth that was the meaningful idea, that resulted in what the paleontologists have identified as fertility goddesses. And we know that for many ancients, certain animals became the ordering metaphors in their search for meaning. Were such notions as these the beginning of the long and varied history of man's religious quest which has, after many millennia, resulted in all of our formulated statements of belief, our creeds, doctrines and "holy" books?

This is what I think I have seen when I have traveled back down this long path that Darwin first charted, all the way to the dawn of human consciousness, when my first ancestor stepped across the evolutionary dividing line: I think I have witnessed the birth of man as a spiritual/religious animal. I have witnessed that birth in the questions I have heard him asking about the meaning of his existence. And I know he is my relative because he was asking the same questions about his existence that I find myself asking about mine. We are one in our quest for meaning. Interestingly, we part company only when he starts giving answers to those questions. I can relate to his need for answers to ease his bewilderment, but not to the specific content of the answers he came up with. I cannot relate to sun gods, fertility gods, snake gods, falcon gods, raven gods, old-man-in-the-sky gods, and all the rest of those tentative embodiments that we have imposed upon our notion of an ultimate reality that lies at the heart of our existence. And what does that say to me about my sense of myself as a spiritual/religious person? It says to me that at the core of my spiritual/religious sensibilities are the questions that I ask, which are the questions that every human being who ever lived has had to confront: Who am I? What am I doing here? What is the meaning of my existence? It is the unchanging and universal questions themselves that define us as spiritual beings, not the specific content of our *answers* to the questions. It is not the factual truth of the answers that we give that establishes the validity of our religious experience, but the depth and authenticity of the questions that we ask. The answers change, have always changed, will always change, as our understanding of the world around us changes. When our answers stop changing and harden into stone, they become idols made in the likeness of ourselves at that particular stage of our development. And when we settle for those answers as the final truth, we are likely to start acting like little gods ourselves. To be fully human, I am convinced, is to be a spiritual/religious animal. To be a spiritual/religious animal is to live even today in the birth pangs of our humanity, to hearken back to the hinging moment when, having found themselves in a wonderful and challenging new world, our first human parents asked themselves, "What is this all about?"

THE DEVIL IN THE MIRROR

What really happened in Eden

ON SUNDAY MORNING, SEPTEMBER 15, 1963, a homemade bomb went off in a window well of the Sixteenth Street Baptist Church in Birmingham, Alabama, killing four little girls who were attending Sunday school. On the following Sunday, I stood in the pulpit of the Mullins Presbyterian Church in Mullins, South Carolina, a tobacco market town of about sixty-five hundred people located in the northeastern corner of the state, and delivered a sermon titled "My Hometown,"[1] in which I claimed my personal share of the guilt for that evil act, as a son of Birmingham, as a son of Alabama, and as a son of the segregated South. The sermon was intended to have more the tone of a confession than of an accusation, but it was clear that, in spreading the responsibility for that crime to rest on the consciences of the broader community, the "broader community" I was implicating included those who sat in the segregated pews in front of me, even though they lived far from the city limits of Birmingham and the state borders of Alabama. My point was taken—if not taken *well*—by the members of my congregation, as one young businessman protested afterward, "You've accused me of murder!"

As a result of what had to be the worst case of bad timing I can imagine, I had been scheduled for months to leave town that very afternoon to attend a two-week clinic at the Presbyterian seminary in Richmond, Virginia. Had I been thinking more clearly or more compassionately, I would surely have canceled that trip in order to attend to the wounds I had opened, but I didn't, and my leaving town gave the inevitable impression of one who had taken his shot and then "cut and run." While I was gone, the elders of the congregation met and voted unanimously to ask for my resignation. On my return, believing that I could never heal the breach that my sermon had exposed, I acceded to their demand, requesting that my resignation be effective at the end of the year in order to have time to make plans for what now seemed to be a very uncertain professional future. Thus, I had three months to live and work in a town where I had become a pariah, a "pinko liberal," a "communist..." I managed to get through that difficult time with the support of my family and a few good friends in the church, but I almost didn't survive what would come a few weeks after that fateful Sunday in September.

Late one afternoon I stopped by the church on my way home for dinner. Our home, the Presbyterian manse, was located diagonally across from the church on Sandy Bluff Road, a secondary artery leading out of town. On such brief stops, I was in the habit of parking on a street that ran beside the church facing away from the main road. Upon leaving, I would just make a U-turn, pause at the stop sign on the corner, turn right onto Sandy Bluff, and then immediately turn left into our driveway. On this particular afternoon, as I locked the door of the dark and empty church and headed for my car, I am not sure what it was that alerted me to another car moving slowly down the side street toward me. Perhaps I was sensitized by the hostile air I had been breathing for the last few weeks. Maybe it was just that its lights were not on in the darkening twilight. Whatever aroused my suspicions, it struck me as ominous that a large sedan full of men (at least five) should be moving so slowly down *that* street in *that* neighborhood at *that* time of day. Something about it just wasn't right. They crept pass me as I reached my own car. Not wanting to alert them to my alarm, I didn't look carefully to see if I could recognize any of the men. As casually as possible I got in and started my engine. By then the other car was at the corner. Had I made my usual U-turn, I would have ended up directly behind the suspicious sedan as it braked for the stop sign and I would have been blocked in. That didn't seem like a good idea. Instead, I drove straight up the street to the next corner, made three right turns, and was back on Sandy Bluff heading for the manse. As I passed the church and the side street intersection at a pretty fast clip, I saw that the other car was still sitting at the corner—a long wait at a stop sign when there was no other traffic about. I turned into our driveway, parked in the carport, and hurried into the house, locking the door behind me. I told Rebecca that something strange was going on and she and I went upstairs to our darkened bedroom. When we looked out of the window, my anxiety took a leap. The large dark car had moved around the corner and was parked directly across the street from the manse, lights off, waiting…for what? Were they going to throw a bomb, or burn a cross? Rebecca was terrified; I was scared and angry; we were defenseless. Our two children, ages seven months and three years, were in their own bedrooms. A call to the police would have been useless; there was no law against parking on a deserted public street. I don't know how long we waited and watched; it could have been thirty minutes, it could have been an hour. It seemed an agonizingly long time. Eventually, however, the car started up and drove away. The immediate threat was over.

What was going on? I was never to know for sure. At the time, we thought of it in terms of a bomb threat (there was much talk of bombs in the South in those days). Over the intervening years, I have dismissed that scenario, but certainly, as far as I was concerned, the men in that car were up to no good. Had they been following me even before I stopped off at the church? Possibly. I was driving a distinctive foreign car, which would have made me easy to spot. Were they Klan members? Quite possibly, maybe even probably. Were they just out to scare me? If so, they would not have accomplished that by merely driving by. What would have happened had I made my usual turn and found myself blocked in at the corner? The spot was isolated from view from nearby houses, and it was getting dark. In my mind's eye I see men piling out of that car, coming at me before I can reverse or get around them. An abduction? Maybe, but I doubt it. I suspect now that the "upstart young liberal preacher" was about to be "taught a lesson," and most likely a painful one. Smashed car windows? (My poor little Italian car!) Broken bones and bruises and a trip to the hospital emergency room? Thankfully, I never found out. One thing I know is that every time I see a "No U-turn" sign, I smile inside. And I also know that in the darkening twilight of that October afternoon, I came very close to a fatal encounter with evil in one of its most palpable and frightening forms.

Who were those men, and why were they out to hurt me or even to kill me or, at the very least, to terrorize my family (they did accomplish that)? They were not the typical Hollywood version of beer-bellied redneck Klansmen driving old pickup trucks. They were in a clean, late model four-door sedan, possibly a Buick (I have always thought that I recognized the car as belonging to a well-known leading citizen of the town, but I couldn't be positive). They were most likely just average family and businessmen of the town, some of whom I might well have known. No doubt on the following Sunday they would be found in their familiar pews in the Baptist or Methodist or perhaps even the Presbyterian Church. Even though I never got a clear look at any of them, I am convinced that they were not some obviously dangerous criminal types, but otherwise law-abiding citizens who believed that what they were attempting to do was necessary and justifiable. I am also convinced that my fear of them was not baseless paranoia; those good citizens might well have done me some serious bodily harm had I not been alert enough to elude their trap. It never happened again. Why they gave up after only one attempt to get at me I could only speculate. Maybe they just lost their nerve. Maybe it was a good thing for their sakes as well as mine that I was able to slip out of their grasp; they might have done something that they would have regretted for the rest of their lives. The odds were that I probably met some of those men again during the last couple of months that I lived in that town. I probably met them on the street or in their places of work or even in church on Sunday, but I would never have recognized them. They were just ordinary people like you and me; they bore no "mark of Cain" that would identify them out as evildoers.

Several years ago Rabbi Harold Kushner published a small book titled *When Bad Things Happen to Good People*[2], which was an admirable effort to bring up to date the question that goes back to the book of Job in the Old Testament and probably as far back as the birth in human consciousness of a sense of moral justice: Why *do* good people suffer unjustly the "slings and arrows of outrageous fortune." If God is a good and loving father, how can he allow his children to be victimized by the schemes of evil men or the forces of capricious nature? That would seem to be one of the great imponderables of human history. There is another question, however, perhaps even more relevant to our modern experience that needs some serious pondering. It is the question that was raised in dramatic form for me on a side street in a small South Carolina tobacco town four decades ago: Why do *good* people do *bad* things? What could cause a group of ordinary, church-going, law-abiding citizens to decide that they should get together and lay a trap for the young minister of one of their town's prominent churches, to catch him off guard, so that they could...beat him up?...kill him?...smash up his car?...terrorize his family?...because of his liberal views on race? Everything about that frightening afternoon indicated that those men were carrying out a carefully plotted plan of attack. Their attempted assault on me was not the result of a sudden emotional outburst. It resulted from a calculated decision made by a group of normally rational men who had time to think about what they were doing and who concluded that it would be a justifiable and necessary act under the circumstances as they understood them. What could have caused them to come to that conclusion? If we could begin to answer that question, we might also gain some insight into some other troubling events that have occurred over the years. Abu Ghraib comes to mind as a recent example. How could a group of U. S. soldiers and marines, presumably just your average American young men and women, turn into torturers and bestial tormentors of the helpless prisoners they were assigned to guard? What could cause these basically good young people to do such a thing? What happens to the educated and talented man who rises to the top of the business world to become CEO of a major corporation, who then allows petty greed to overwhelm his judgment to the extent that he is willing to cheat his employees out of their life savings and risk destroying the very company that has made him rich, just so he can have more of what he already has in abundance? He obviously wasn't stupid, and I don't believe he set out with some criminal intent to steal, but neither could he legitimately claim that it was all a mistake. So what made him do it? Then of course, there is the Holocaust, the infamous program instituted as official government policy by one of the most highly educated and cultured nations in the world for the systematic extermination of six million "undesirable" members of its own society. How could the good citizens of that great "Christian" nation have done this awful thing or condoned it or looked the other way as their neighbors were taken away to the trains for "resettlement in the east."

None of the examples of evil acts and inhumane deeds that I have cited came about solely as a result of the machinations and schemes of obviously depraved or demonic individuals. Neither the men who plotted their attack on me, nor the people who populated that town, whose majority opinions regarding racial matters provided those men the context that seemed to justify their plan, were anything but ordinary, basically law-abiding citizens. How do we explain that? Those young people who let themselves be photographed torturing and humiliating the prisoners at Abu Ghraib were not unique in their depravity. They were not inhuman monsters. There was something strangely naive and almost childishly innocent about those horrible pictures, as if they thought that what they were engaged in was some sort of a game. How do we account for this? Those men who robbed those hundreds and hundreds of hard working people of their life savings and brought down those hugely influential corporations were not evil demons. They were highly respected, basically well-intentioned businessmen and community leaders. They were the very icons of the American success story. How are we to understand what went so wrong? The people who elected Adolph Hitler to be Chancellor of Germany did not put him in office so that he could initiate a program to exterminate six million Jews. They elected him to restore a sense of pride and dignity to a nation badly defeated in World War I, unjustly humiliated by the terms of the armistice imposed by the victorious allies, and suffering from the further deprivations brought on by an international economic depression. They desperately wanted a leader who would lift the country out of despair and hopelessness, and he seemed to be the one. When they applauded Hitler for his great dream of a strong and racially pure Germany, they could not yet have imagined the death camps that would turn out to be an integral part of that dream. How could that rather innocent hope for a good and great nation have produced the monstrous killing machine that it became?

I would suggest that one of the reasons such questions are so troubling and so difficult for us to comprehend is that our Western religious tradition has failed to equip its adherents with an adequate explanation for the presence of evil in the world, and I would suggest further that that failure represents perhaps the single greatest shortcoming of Western Christianity. In its basic teachings, when it has been called upon to explain why human beings are capable of committing unspeakable crimes against each other, even when they know better, the Christian Church has given, at best, an inadequate and shallow response, and the explanations it has given have adversely tinctured our whole Western outlook on life for almost two thousand years. Because the

Christian Church and its doctrines have so dominated the intellectual and moral life of the West for so long, even the attitudes and behavior of nonbelievers, the whole culture—the way we think about our lives—has been affected by the Church's overly simplistic formula for what is wrong with the human species, with its emphasis on individual sin and guilt, rewards and punishment, salvation and damnation. I believe that Christianity's interpretation of the negative side of human experience has been off the mark from the very beginning. The philosopher, Bertrand Russell, a staunch exponent of the optimism of the Enlightenment and its attitudes regarding human destiny, was once criticized by the economist John Maynard Keynes, who said that Russell's views on life and human affairs were "brittle" because they had "no solid diagnosis of human nature underlying them." The Church's analysis of the problem of evil suffers from the same kind of superficiality; it lacks a "solid diagnosis of human nature."[3]

If the reader will bear with me, let me reiterate what that essential teaching has been as the Church has presented it over the centuries. This is briefly what I learned from a life in the Church, from years of Sunday school lessons, the catechisms, college religion courses, and divinity school theological studies:

When God created our original biological ancestors, whose proper names were Adam and Eve, he gave them for a home a place called the Garden of Eden (supposedly located, according to some biblical archeologists, somewhere in the Fertile Crescent between the Tigris and Euphrates rivers in modern day Iraq). It was a paradise, a perfect place where everything was provided for them. There they could live in perfect tranquility and innocence, eating freely of the fruits of the garden (the matter of whether or not they killed the animals of the garden for protein is not mentioned. Chalk one up for the vegetarians!). Being "fruitful" themselves and multiplying was their only task. There was, however, one little hitch in this idyllic plan. There was one fruit that grew in the garden that they were forbidden to eat. It is not usually made clear in the telling of the story just why this rule was put in, perhaps merely as a test of their obedience, though neither is it clear just why God would feel this to be necessary. At any rate, because there was such an abundance available to them, this one exception was hardly enough to cast a shadow over their perfect world. That is until Satan, the Devil, the Evil One (no explanation for what he was doing in this perfect paradise) comes along in the guise of a serpent to tempt them to disobey. He shows the "forbidden fruit" to Eve and describes its delectability, and, for some reason, she chooses to have a bite in direct disobedience of God's command. Then, because she doesn't wish to be alone in her crime, she shows the fruit to Adam and he also chooses to disobey. And that was the end of their perfect and idyllic life.

God catches them in their guilt and drives them out of paradise, and because they have committed this initial act of disobedience all of their descendants, including us, share in their guilt. We suffer from their same condition, which is called "original sin," and that is why we continue to do bad things. There is nothing we can do about it. We are helpless sinners and unless a way is found to break the cycle of disobedience in which we are caught because of our ancestors' initial rebellion, we will go to eternal punishment when we die. Of course, God later gave Moses the Ten Commandments to show us how to live, but because we continually fail to live up to their precepts, the law only condemns us further. Alas, what are we to do?

Do not despair; there is a way out. Finally, after putting up with his rebellious children for thousands of years (why did it take him so long?), apparently out of a kind of divine frustration with his creation, God takes the extreme step of sending His own son, Jesus, to earth to save us. Jesus takes a stab at teaching us how we ought to live, but, in the end, because only extreme measures will suffice, he offers himself up as a sacrifice for our sins. He dies in our place so that we can be saved. Because he is perfect and without sin, he is able to take on the punishment we deserve. Our guilt is wiped out and we are freed. All we have to do is believe in him, accept his perfect sacrifice on our behalf, and we will go to heaven when we die.

That's pretty much the story as I got it from my years in the Church, and I had no problem with all of that until I found myself as a young preacher having to make sense of it from the pulpit. After all, that was how I saw my task as a preacher (or, according to my official title in the Presbyterian Church, a "teaching elder"): to make relevant sense for modern people of Christian doctrine, which is based upon the biblical story. I found myself in trouble trying to make sense for them out of things that didn't make a lot of sense to me. I remember, in the days leading up to the Easter season, agonizing over what I could say about the crucifixion of Jesus. What did it mean to say that he died for us? In what sense was his death a sacrifice for *my* sins, an atonement for *my* guilt? If I am awaiting death in the gas chamber for a capital crime I have committed, and some innocent person convinces the authorities to let him take my place, that might be very nice for me, but in what way does it affect my guilt for what I have done? In what way did Jesus' dying on the cross have anything directly to do with me, any more than any other martyr's death, Martin Luther King's or Abraham Lincoln's or Mahatma Ghandi's? If God is a loving father who forgives his children, then why was all of this sacrificing of his son on the cross necessary? As far as "original sin" is concerned, what kind of genetics of guilt did God invent that I should bear the blame for what my ancient ancestors had done? I am not guilty for what my own father did. Oh, I might suffer for what he did. My children might suffer if he failed to pass on to me good parenting skills, but the only thing of which I am individually guilty that is remotely connected to him is my own failure to fulfill my responsibility as a parent. So, what's this business about "original sin"?

Troubled by such questions (I was troubled by a lot of other questions, but, for now, let's stick to the one about "original sin" and what to do about it) I decided one day to go back and read anew the original story in Genesis of the fall of Adam and Eve and of their expulsion from paradise. Perhaps the years I had spent away from any religious

137

involvement had afforded me a fresh perspective, for when I reread it, I received quite a shock. It was not at all the story I had learned, and it certainly was not the same story that popular religious tradition would have us believe. If this story was the source of the Church's teaching about sin and damnation, it had gotten it all wrong.

The story of the so-called temptation and fall is found in the third chapter of Genesis. Before we read it afresh, however, there are a few things we need to consider as a sort of preamble. First of all, we need to be clear that what we have here is not a piece of factual narrative history and the characters in the story are not actual historic persons (we're not talking now about whether the story is *true* or not, but what *kind* of truth it is). This is a mythological tale, a fable, a legend, the kind of story invented by ancient people, probably passed down from generation to generation, as part of their oral tradition long before it was written down. As such, its function was to transmit the collective wisdom of a people about their origins. It is a wonderfully dramatic story, with all the earmarks of a classic fable—even a talking animal—which were short tales that taught lessons about life. "Who are we? Where do we come from? What are we doing here? It was to address these kinds of questions that such tales as this originated and took their places in the collective memory of ancient peoples.

As for the cast of characters in this little drama, there are four (in order of appearance): the Serpent (at no point is he identified as Satan or the Devil), the Woman, her Husband, and God (who only appears late in the drama to sort of wrap things up after the main action has occurred). At no point in this part of the Genesis myth are the names Adam and Eve used; in fact, the word "Eve" occurs for the first time only after the story of the expulsion from the garden. Neither "Adam" nor "Eve" are proper names for individual persons such as are, for instance, "Joseph" and "Mary." "Adam" is the generic Hebrew word for *man* or *mankind*, and "Eve" in Hebrew means something like *mother of all living.* "Adam" and "Eve" are, thus, not intended as names for historic individuals who actually existed and were called by those names; they are rather symbolic characters representing our generic ancestors from out of the mists of prehistory.

Now, on to the story itself. (One further note: as you read it, be aware that the voice of the Serpent can probably best be understood as the Woman talking with herself, the voice of her own doubts about the conditions of her existence.)

> *Now the serpent was more subtle than any other wild creature that the Lord God had made. He said to the woman, "Did God say, you shall not eat of any tree of the garden?"*
>
> *And the woman said to the serpent, "We may eat of the fruit of the trees of the garden; but God said, you shall not eat of the fruit of the tree which is in the midst of the garden, neither shall you touch it, lest you die."*
>
> *But the serpent said to the woman, "You will not die. For God knows that when you eat of it your eyes will be opened, and you will be like God, knowing good and evil."*

> *So, when the woman saw that the tree was good*
> *for food, and that it was a delight to the eyes, and*
> *that the tree was to be desired to make one wise, she*
> *took of its fruit and ate; and she also gave some to her*
> *husband and he ate.*
>
> *Then the eyes of both of them were opened and*
> *they knew that they were naked; and they sewed fig*
> *leaves together and made themselves aprons.*

Genesis 3:1–7 (R.S.V.)

As the Judeo-Christian religious tradition came to dominate Western civilization, this ancient mythological tale served as a primary source for the explanation of how wrongdoing and evil were introduced into the world. However, the interpretation of the story that came to be the basis for the Christian Church's teaching about sin and the need for salvation, and which has become the stuff of popular religious belief—with the Devil in the guise of a snake tempting Eve with the apple that God has forbidden her and her husband to eat, their disobedience, their expulsion from paradise, and our inheritance of their original sin—is so simplistic and morally shallow that it misses almost entirely the subtlety and force of the essential story. Taken literally, as a narrative about a simple act of disobedience, it makes very little sense. So, what were the ancient mythmakers really trying to tell us? Surely the key to understanding the story is the identity of the so-called forbidden fruit. It wasn't just that it was forbidden that made it attractive. The Woman and her Husband in this story were not like willful children disobeying just for the sake of asserting themselves. No, it was the nature of the fruit itself that struck their fancy. And it certainly was not the apple of popular folklore. It was the fruit of a very special tree, the tree of the knowledge of good and evil—the tree of moral discernment. If they ate its fruit, their eyes would be opened as they had not been opened prior to this moment. Knowing good and evil, they could now make choices about their lives. They would understand things they could not have grasped before, and so they would be like God, new kinds of creatures, unlike any others in the garden. All of this made that particular fruit very desirable for food, and so, as the story goes, they ate.

I believe this "tale of temptation" is actually a story about the moment when humans first became fully human. The eating of the fruit from the symbolic tree of knowledge represents the moment of awakening, when a threshold was crossed and our first human ancestors recognized themselves as different from all the other creatures with whom they shared their earthly residence. We know, of course, that the awakening of *Homo sapiens* only happened very gradually and that there was not a single "moment" when their eyes were suddenly opened to the truth about themselves. Nevertheless, however slowly the dawning may have occurred, there came a time when our early ancestors knew that they were unique in the world, and one of the first things they must have felt was the ambiguity of their situation. What were they? Who were they? They were not just animals any longer, certainly, and yet they still experienced the limitations of animal existence. They still had to eat to live, needed shelter from the cold and wet, were driven by sexual craving, defecated like any other creature, and experienced pain...but for the first time, they had looked up from these mundane physical aspects of their lives to experience the wonder of the world around them and to question their place in it. Though stuck within the exigencies of animal existence, their minds and their spirits soared. They found to their own wonder that they could project themselves beyond the immediate demands of the moment to imagine what could happen in the future, which gave them immense new powers over their environment and over the other animals that lacked that capacity. This capacity to imagine their own futures also enabled them to envision something else that had never been thought of before. They could see, in the future, their own deaths. They had stumbled upon one of the great paradoxes of *Homo sapien* life. Humans were the first animals to know that they were animals! They were the first animals with the capacity for self-knowledge and, therefore, the first animals to know that they were going to die—to know the ultimate limitation imposed on animal life. They were the first to contemplate the implications of that hard fact and the first to have a choice as to how they would deal with it.

Could there be a more poignant dramatization of the ambiguity experienced by those early humans than the comical picture of Adam and Eve awkwardly scurrying about to gather fig leaves and crudely stitching them together for aprons to cover their private parts? For the first time, they were aware of their nakedness and were embarrassed by it. Animals are not troubled by their nakedness; they feel no embarrassment at being animals with their genitals exposed for everyone to see. According to the mythmakers' telling of the story, our first parents had eaten the fruit that had opened their eyes and allowed them to know what it is to be like God. Unfortunately for them, eating the fruit didn't actually make them gods or angels. They didn't become some kind of ethereal spirits with ideal bodies. They were still the same lumpy, hairy, physical creatures they had always been, but now they felt the contradiction between their kinship with the animals and their new spiritual and moral freedom, and they were troubled by it. They were anxious in a way they had never been before they symbolically "ate the forbidden fruit" and took that fateful step into full humanity.

The story ends with their expulsion from the garden. No, that is wrong! The human story *begins* with their expulsion from the garden. The garden is the innocence of pre-human animal existence. *Homo sapiens* does not live in the innocence of paradise, where everything is provided and his only task is to propagate the species, and where there is no freedom and there are no choices more complicated than which fruit he shall eat today. He has moved into a whole new world. The story of Adam and Eve and their expulsion from the Garden of Eden is not the story of what has been labeled original sin. That is where the Church and its teaching has gotten it wrong. This is not the day of man's fall; this is graduation day! The eating of the fruit of the tree of knowledge has nothing *directly* to do with "sin" or "evil"; it has to do with the birth of moral awareness and the freedom of choice. This old mythological tale, which has come to be known erroneously as the story of the "temptation and fall of man," is simply a wonderfully imaginative (even with a touch of the comic—I can hear someone like Billy Crystal doing the voice of the serpent!) and beautifully poetic dramatization of the birth of *Homo sapiens*. This is the Old Testament's symbolic version of human evolution.

So, then, what does all of this have to do with the question with which we started: why do good people do bad things? I believe that the answer to that question can be found in the intersection of two fundamental truths about human life and behavior. The first of those truths is that…

EVERYTHING THAT WE DO AND EVERY CHOICE THAT WE MAKE IS PART OF OUR EFFORT TO GET THROUGH LIFE WITH THE GREATEST DEGREE OF SATISFACTION AND THE LEAST AMOUNT OF PAIN.

I believe that it can be stated unequivocally that there is nothing that we choose to do throughout our lives—notwithstanding the ultimate results of some of our choices—that does not *originate* from that basic pursuit of happiness. Our primary motivation in life, from the moment of our birth, has been to satisfy our physical and emotional needs and to avoid as much pain as possible, and it is against the backdrop of that underlying impulse that we make all of our decisions and all of our choices. We may be mistaken about what will really bring us the satisfaction we seek, but that is what we're after. We want comfort and harmony and the fulfillment of our needs and desires, and we want to avoid suffering and discord and frustration. The original motive for an armed robber doing what he does is not just to harm other people and it certainly is not to turn himself into a miserable, hunted creature. On the contrary, he does what he does because he mistakenly believes that getting money by this means will make him happy. Oh, he may come to love, for its own sake, the sense of power that he gets from forcing other people to give him their possessions, but even this is part of his effort to satisfy his need to feel good about himself, to feel strong and powerful. The white-collar criminal who embezzles money from his employer is usually doing so because he thinks he needs the money for some good reason, and even if he is partly driven by a grudge against his boss because of some real or imagined injustice, he is still basically trying to get rid of the pain in his own life. The abusive husband who beats his wife does so because his own doubts about his masculinity are so hurtful to his sense of well-being that he must find some kind of relief from that pain. So, I believe it is possible to say—without attempting to justify the results of our decisions—that, at least in terms of original intent, everything we are trying to do at any juncture derives from a basically good motive, and that goes for everyone, everywhere, all of the time, no exceptions.

The second fundamental truth about ourselves that bears directly upon how we act and why we do what we do is that…

EVERY ONE OF US EXPERIENCES THE SAME AMBIGUITY ABOUT OUR LIVES THAT OUR EARLIEST ANCESTORS FELT WHEN THEY FIRST STEPPED ACROSS THE THRESHOLD INTO FULL HUMANNESS.

That is what we inherited from our original forebears, not original sin, but original ambiguity. Like our first ancestors who, when their "eyes were opened," were confronted by the contradictory nature of their situation, we, too, find ourselves caught in the tug-of-war between our animal limitations and our spiritual yearnings. Like them, we often find ourselves wondering just who we are. An identity crisis is something only human beings experience. We do indeed seem to be like gods. How could a mere mortal compose a Bach cantata, carve Michelangelo's *David*, envision and built Chartres Cathedral, conceive a mathematical formula (like $E=MC^2$) that explains so much about our expanding universe, first imagine traveling into outer space and then build the vehicles that make it happen, give birth in the mind to metaphors that connect us to eternity? The wily serpent in the myth of Eden was right when he told our first parents that if they would eat of the forbidden fruit of full humanity they would be like God. The problem is that we, like them, do not wear our "godness" with confidence. We look at ourselves and, like those two characters in the mythmaker's tale, we are embarrassed by what we see; we don't want our animal equipment exposed to everyone's gaze. That part of our nature seems somehow beneath the dignity of creatures such as we who now populate this "brave new world." And then there is that other thing that looms over us. In spite of the power of our minds and the quality of our spirits, we keep running up against the restraints of our mortality. As we grow older, our bodies begin to fail us, usually at a time when our spirits and minds are at the height of their capacities, and we know that our time is running out. When we allow ourselves to think about it, our own deaths and the deaths of those we most love and need drape like a pall over all of our dreams and endeavors. Death comes so often as a rude cancellation notice that leaves so much that is good unfinished, and we are constantly being reminded of the precariousness of our own existence. It frightens us and offends our sense of justice when we hear of a brilliant young scientist, or an accomplished artist, or a parent of young children, whose promise is yet unshaped being snuffed out by unexpected disease or something as mindlessly stupid as a drunk driver's criminal recklessness. The daily news is a persistent reminder of our vulnerability. Vulnerability! Not exactly a godlike trait. We are indeed still caught on the horns of the dilemma that baffled and troubled our original progenitors. As Thomas More put it so poetically, "a piece of the sky and a chunk of the earth lies lodged in the heart of every human being."[4] Much has changed over the thousands and thousands of years since *Homo erectus* looked up from the ground and walked out of the "garden of innocence" across the threshold of human history to become *Homo sapiens*, but this one thing has not changed: we still live with his "original ambiguity." That is Adam's true bequest, not a sinful nature, just a contradictory one.

In the last chapter, I suggested that one cannot understand man's spiritual and religious nature without some grasp of what happened to our earliest ancestors as they woke up to their new situation on the human side of the hinge of evolution. Likewise, I believe that it is not possible to understand fully "what went wrong" with us without also returning to that early morning of our human experience.

This is what those ancient mythmakers of Eden glimpsed even without the clarifying insights of evolutionary science. It is just terribly unfortunate that the Christian Church has so sadly misunderstood their story. I wonder if the early Church fathers' interpretation of Adam's fall from grace, which leads to the scenario of individual sin and damnation, and our guilt and need of redemption were not also part of their effort to ensure the success of the young Institutional Church. I mean, if you convince people that they are guilty sinners and then get them to believe that their only hope for salvation lies in the grace available to them through the sacraments of the Church, they will become dependent upon the Church in a way that guarantees its importance in their lives and its success as an institution. Certainly the Church has spent a lot of energy over the last two millennia making people feel guilty. It is a shame to have put so much blame on that first generation of our human family for their original sin, which they supposedly passed on to us when all they were trying to do was to cope with the contradictions and ambiguities of their new situation.

And that is what we've been doing ever since we departed Eden. Like our first parents, we have been trying to find happiness and satisfaction and peace in spite of the fundamentally frustrating ambiguity of our situation. And how we go about doing that is *the* critical issue, I am convinced, that determines what kind of humans we will be, both as individuals and as societies. Indeed, I believe (and this is the third big "truth" about us that follows from the two above) that...

THERE IS NOTHING THAT OCCURS IN THE WORLD THAT HAS BEEN CALLED EVIL OR IMMORAL OR IN-HUMAN OR WHAT THE CHURCH CALLS SINFUL THAT DOES NOT RESULT, DIRECTLY OR INDIRECTLY, FROM OUR ANXIOUS EFFORTS TO OVERCOME THE BASIC AMBIGUITIES AND CONTRADICTIONS INHERENT IN OUR HUMAN SITUATION.

That's a pretty bold statement, I know, but I believe it is true, and the implications of that truth are enormous, especially in the light of how we Westerners have learned to think about the problem of evil in the world. It does not mean that there is no such thing as evil, or that its presence in the world is merely an illusion. It does not mean that what is immoral is so simply in the eye of the beholder. It does not mean that what is wrong in human behavior is just a matter of opinion. It *does* mean that what we, in the past, have called evil or immoral or inhuman or sinful behavior is the product of a very human response to a predicament in which every one of us is caught. As far as root causes are concerned, the differences between moral and immoral behavior are far more subtle than we would like to think; it's far more difficult to determine clearly just who the good guys and the bad guys are. And it means that the problem of evil in the world is entirely man-made. There is no devil out there who "made me do it!" The "Devil" or "Satan" or whatever we choose to call that common personification of evil, is a figment of our imagination, invented, I'm afraid, by us humans as a way to avoid our own responsibility for whatever has gone wrong in the world. Whatever evil I have done had its origin right here inside of me as a result of my own anxieties and the anxieties that have become incorporated in our society (more about that later). Pogo Possum, the cartoon character, said it as well as any philosopher or theologian ever could: "We have met the enemy and he is us."[5] If you want to see the Devil, all you have to do is look in the mirror.

As for "sin," I think we would do well to drop that word from our vocabulary entirely, because there is nothing that occurs on the stage of human activity or in the world of human relationships that is adequately described by that term as it has come to be used in the Western world. The difference between good and evil, moral behavior and immoral behavior is not simply a matter of good acts and bad acts. It cannot be summarized by a legalistic catalog of transgressions, conveniently divided into "venial sins" and "mortal sins," that covers all the possibilities of being bad for which one might feel a need to be forgiven. Living a good life is not merely a matter of obeying the rules laid down in a book of moral etiquette that tells one what to do and what not to do in any given situation. Our simplistic use of the word "sin" to describe wrongdoing misses the truth that any act, however innocent seeming or well intended, is capable of being corrupted by the mixed motives of the actor. My most loving and generous deed can be changed into something less than righteous by my need to be seen doing it so that I will be admired as one who is a step above the ordinary folks. As a matter of fact—and this is one of the great ironies of human experience—most of what we call evil or immoral or sinful originates not from some twisted need on the part of some people to be *bad*, but, quite the contrary, from our universal need to be *good*, to feel good about ourselves and to be admired and respected by others. No one is trying to be bad, or to feel bad about him or herself. We all want to be good.

The problem arises when we start to measure our goodness. How do we know when we are being good? Or at least when we are being good enough? Good enough to be loved and respected by others? Good enough to get the approval of our parents, of society, of God? How do we overcome the sense of incompleteness and inadequacy that so often plagues us? What measuring stick shall we use to determine our success as a person deserving of love and respect? We could measure our performance against some perfect ideal of human behavior, some philosophical definition of the good life. Or we could guage our success by our compliance to that exhortation I was taught in Sunday School: "Be ye perfect even as your Father in heaven is perfect." But those kinds of comparisons are not exactly calculated to make one feel good about oneself. None of us comes out so well in a contest with perfection. So we do the next best thing. We make ourselves feel good about ourselves by comparison to others. As the lead character in Ian McEwen's novel, *Atonement*, concluded, "Finally, you had to measure yourself by other people; there really was nothing else."[6]

I believe that if we listen very carefully, we will hear, reverberating from within the sound of every violent, abusive, jealous, ambitiously manipulative, proudly self-promoting, or greedy act, the anxious voice of the perpetrator screaming in silent supplication, "I just want to feel good about myself!" And what is wrong with that? But then, the problem is not with the goal; the problem lies in what one does to achieve that goal. We are all trying to get comfortable with the inherent contradictions that are simply part of being human. We are all trying to overcome the anxieties that stem from the conflicts we experience as self-conscious animals. And everything we do is colored by that need to erase the gap between our spiritual and animal selves. There is nothing that we do, however morally respectable or well intentioned or socially approved that is not subject to being used by us to promote our own position and prestige in comparison to others, and over the heads of others. How useful was that velvet paneled black robe with its colored stoles I wore as I mounted the pulpit on Sunday mornings for providing me a sense of my uniqueness in contrast to regular people. What a sense of power it gives one to stand in that high pulpit looking down at the congregation gathered below. There is nothing that we do—there is no situation in which we find ourselves—that does not present us with a mixed bag of moral possibilities. Of course, that is not what the moralist wants to hear. He wants a clearer division between good and evil. He wants the world of human behavior to be neatly defined by simple moral rules. He wants to believe that posting the Ten Commandments in every county courthouse will make us a better-behaved people. He wants to know for sure, at every turn, what is good and what is bad. I had a Bible professor my freshman year in college whose course workbook began with this sentence: "There are two kinds of people in the world: good people and bad people." I'm sorry, professor, but it isn't quite that simple.

Go back now to where we started this chapter, to my encounter with that carload of anonymous men who terrorized my family and most likely intended to do even worse. Who were they and what made them decide to come after me in the twilight of that autumn afternoon in that small Southern town? I have already suggested that they were not some red-necked rabble, but most likely just your ordinary town citizens, family men, businessmen, church goers. Nor were they driven by some uncontrollably furious reaction to the sermon I had preached. At least a month, maybe even longer, had passed since that Sunday. I had already resigned and was basically a lame duck as far as any influence I might have had in the church or the community was concerned. They had had plenty of time to consider their feelings about what I had said from the pulpit and what they ought to do about it. And they had apparently decided, after consideration and consultation, that a violent act was called for. What brought them to that conclusion? Why do good people like these do bad things such as they were planning to do?

As calculated as their actions seem to have been, those men were scared to the very core of their beings. They were scared in the way that James Baldwin described in his letter to his nephew published on the one hundredth anniversary of the emancipation: "Try to imagine how you would feel if you woke up one morning to find the sun shining and all the stars aflame. You would be frightened because it is out of the order of nature. Any upheaval in the universe is terrifying because it so profoundly attacks one's sense of one's own reality. Well, the black man has functioned in the white man's world as a fixed star, as an immovable pillar: and as he moves out of his place, heaven and earth are shaken to their foundations."[7] The men in that car were going through an upheaval in their universe, a shaking of their very foundations. They were men who had bought into, or more accurately, been *born* into, a social system based on racial segregation, which was the enforcement of a deep seated and unquestioned belief in the natural superiority of the white man over the black man. They had learned that a black man "comes to your back door instead of your front door." They had never known any other way of living; it was the way their world was built. And now a "fixed star" in their universe had begun to move and they felt themselves, their community, their whole system of values to be under attack. They desperately needed some way to strike back, and I was an obvious target because I had let myself be the voice of the change that was so profoundly threatening to their very sense of reality. It wasn't me personally they were after. They were attacking what they saw as an evil that was menacing their very way of life. And that, to them, was a necessary, and therefore a good thing, to do. They were trying to do something they believed was good.

It is important to note that these men were not the originators of their own racism. Racists they surely were, but their racism was inherited. It was not born of their individual feelings of racial superiority. They had those feelings, certainly, but they didn't come by them because they were individually perverse and depraved bigots. The sociologist, James Loewen, defines one of the present-day legacies of slavery as "the cultural racism it instilled in whites."[8] Those good citizens were already "cultural racists" long before they were individually guilty of racist feelings and attitudes. From the moments of their births, they had been socialized into a segregated society, been taught to know who they were by the color of their skin, and to believe that their skin color gave them a natural right to social dominance. Certainly the evil of racial discrimination is one of the clearer examples of our individual human tendency to make ourselves feel better about ourselves by looking down on those whom we choose to think of as inferior. Its origins surely are to be found somewhere way back in human history after differences in skin tone had evolved (probably because of geographical dispersion) and a fair skinned individual first looked upon those with darker skins and discovered that it made him feel good about himself that he was not like one of them. But racism is also a prime example of how an evil can become incorporated into the very structures of a society and a culture.

The young businessman who reacted to my sermon on the Birmingham bombing with the vehement protest that I had accused him of murder was wrong. I did not accuse him of murder. He was not a murderer and I knew that; he was a neighbor of mine. What I *did* accuse him of—though I had tried hard to avoid sounding accusatory—was that he and I and all the good white citizens of Birmingham and of Alabama and of the segregated South, which included the citizens of Mullins, South Carolina, and the members of that all-white Presbyterian congregation, had been willing participants in, had tolerated, if not actively supported, a social system based on racial discrimination. And because that social arrangement was fundamentally unjust and based upon a lie, it had bred mistrust, anger and hatred, and ultimately the kind of fear that had resulted in the bomb that killed those four little girls. Because we lived in that kind of society and we benefited—even if indirectly—from its inequities, we also shared in the responsibility for that crime. That was an idea that he found, and many still find, hard to swallow. The notion of cultural racism, a form of "corporate" evil, and the idea of corporate responsibility (and by implication, of corporate guilt) is a concept that we in the West have a difficult time coming to terms with. And part of the reason that concept is so hard for us to grasp is that, as I suggested earlier, our Western religious tradition has fallen short in its diagnosis of what it is that ails us as a species.

The model by which the Christian Church has traditionally sought to define evil, and on which it has based its moral teachings, is that of the individual whose willful misdeeds (like Eve's disobedience in eating the forbidden fruit) makes him or her personally and individually a sinner deserving of punishment. Even though we are all somehow inheritors of the "original sin" of our first parents, making us subject to the influence of Satan, or the Devil, it is the individual's choice to "yield to temptation" and the individual's sinful acts that separate him or her from God. The Church's mission, then, becomes to convert those individual miscreants, convincing them that they are sinners (making them feel guilty), and "bringing them to Christ." If they will each accept Jesus as their personal savior, believing in the crucifixion as a sacrifice in payment for their personal wrongdoings, they will receive God's forgiveness and become part of Christ's family. Thus will the Kingdom of Heaven be ushered in, one redeemed sinner at a time. Now that is, admittedly, an over simplification of Christian teaching, but it, nevertheless, pretty much sums up the Church's basic message, certainly from the point of view of the Protestant/ Evangelical tradition in which I was nurtured.

The problem with that scenario is that its definition of human depravity, purely in terms of individual sins and individual guilt for individual acts of disobedience, is far too simplistic to account for the depth and complexity of the evil that perennially claws at the fabric of society. Racism, for instance, cannot be fully understood merely as the feelings and attitudes of individual bigots who need to build up their own self-esteem by looking down upon people of other races. It is more like an infectious disease that invades whole communities, whole societies, whole cultures. It is a very subtle disease whose onset is often hardly noticeable. Indeed, it often reaches epidemic proportions before those infected are even aware that they have it, and by that time, it can be so widespread that to the infected victim, the disease itself seems normal. And it is highly contagious, usually being quietly passed on from generation to generation. One of its most grievous effects is a blurring of vision, which prevents its victims from discerning in people around them the fine distinctions of individual personalities and personal traits, causing them to see their neighbors in broad categories of race, nationality, class, or culture. When infectious racism takes a firm hold, it can be so pervasive as to determine how everything in a community is organized, and can become so rigidly normal as a way of life that, to many, the disease is less threatening than the cure. Those good citizens who came after me on that evening long ago had grown up in a culture ravaged by the disease of racism, and though one may fairly judge that they had a worse case than some, there was no one in that town who was not infected to some degree. It was the community's general sickness that allowed those men to believe that they had its tacit approval to commit a violent act. We all know that a person will do things as part of a group that he wouldn't dare to do alone. Not one of those men would have acted against me by himself. And the five of them would not have done what they tried to do had they not believed that there was a crowd behind them.

Likewise, the Holocaust was too big and too complicated a phenomenon to be put down as the work of a few demonstrably evil men. The so-called Final Solution was an enormous national undertaking that required thousands of active participants, as well as the tacit approval of thousands more who merely looked the other way. It wasn't carried out just by military men who could later claim that they were "only following orders." It was the work of file clerks and bureaucrats who kept the records, and efficiency experts who supervised the gathering up of the program's "subjects." It was the work of transportation officials who marshaled all of those seemingly endless lines of cattle cars, and of train crews who kept them running on time to their final destinations. It was the work of those who designed and built the camps, and of those who supplied the materiel that kept them running. What did the industrialists who owned the factories that manufactured those specialized crematory ovens think they were making? What of the chemical companies who supplied the gas that fueled the ovens, as well as that other gas that flowed from those ingenious "shower heads" in the camps' "public baths"? Was their contribution to the effort just business as usual? We have always been staggered by the size of the Final Solution's "success": six million individual human beings systematically gathered from all over Europe and murdered. I imagine, however, that we would be even more overwhelmed if we could ever know the exact number of ordinary people from ordinary walks of life (and from countries other than Germany) who were actively engaged in making the system work. The Holocaust could never have happened without the daily routine work of thousands of private citizens, secretaries, clerks, accountants, drivers, factory workers, plant managers, and food suppliers, who were just concentrating on their specific jobs, the attention to small details enabling them to avoid seeing the big ugly picture, of which they were but tiny parts. And then, in the background, were all those others who thought that purifying society by cleansing it of its "undesirables" was not, after all, such a bad idea. I don't believe that such an enormous undertaking could have succeeded if the Nazis had not found a fertile ground in which to sow their poisonous seeds. Hitler and his henchmen could not have brought to fruition their infamous "solution" to the "Jewish Problem" if a large portion of European society had not already believed there *was* a Jewish Problem. If there had not already been a receptive seedbed of anti-Semitism (widely tolerated, if not actively encouraged by much of European Christendom), the Nazi regime's search for scapegoats on whom to blame the nation's ills would have found far fewer fields from which to gather its bitter harvest. Anti-Semitism is, after all, just another form of the disease of racism, but a peculiarly virulent mutation because it is backed up by deep-seated religious prejudice. And it was a society widely infected by the pernicious disease of anti-Semitic racism that provided the context for the realization of Adolph Hitler's twisted vision. It was that same communal disease that deadened the sensitivities of the Allies, the people of the United States and Great Britain, allowing them to ignore the obvious signs of a burgeoning nightmare, and causing the allied governments to delay taking the steps that might have prevented it. I believe that in a very real sense the whole Christian West must share the guilt for the Holocaust, because that virulent anti-Semitic form of racism is a peculiar child of Christianity, which the Church has never shown the depth of understanding or the moral courage to claim as its own. And I believe that we will never fully grasp what the Holocaust was all about until the Christian Church acknowledges its part in helping to spread the social disease that ultimately led to the wholesale slaughter of those millions of Jews.

Nor will the stain of Abu Ghraib be expunged from the recent pages of the American story by the mere court-martialing of a handful of low-ranking servicemen and women. Those ugly photographs were not portraits of a few bad apples; they were the pictures of a whole enterprise gone badly awry. Finding themselves in a war whose purposes were ill defined, against an enemy who was largely unrecognizable, in a part of the world whose people, culture, and religion were totally alien to them, those few sadly confused, frightened, and frustrated soldiers and marines were able to do what they did because they were apparently under the impression that no one would really care if they took out their frustrations by torturing and dehumanizing a bunch of "rag heads"—who were probably terrorists anyway—neither their superior officers, the higher-ups in Washington, nor a large portion of the American people. And they were not far wrong.

Even the sins of those business tycoons who managed to bring down their huge corporations and with them the economic futures of hundreds of workers cannot be fully explained simply in terms of individual greed and thievery. Of course, the men who were convicted of fraud and insider trading and cooking the books of those financial empires were individually responsible for their decisions and their devastating consequences. But when you start to ask *why* those paragons of American economic success and social prominence would allow themselves to risk destroying the companies they had built, the jobs and futures of their employees, and ultimately their own futures just to enlarge their already overflowing bank accounts, you have to widen the search for an explanation beyond the moral lapses of a few greedy individuals. These were not inherently evil men. On the contrary, they were passionate pursuers of the American Dream. They were the true believers in that other American "religion," which teaches that making money is a virtue in itself, that financial wealth is synonymous with success, and that a person's value in the community is measured by the size of his bank account. So how fair is it for us to single out those practitioners of that faith for being a bit too zealous in their pursuit of it? We had already ordained them as high priests of the sacred institution of American Business. We had rewarded them with all the benefits of community approbation and social status. Should we really have been surprised and self-righteously indignant when we learned that they had gotten a bit too hungry for more of what our culture had been telling them all along they deserved to have?

Defining evil is fairly simple when we think of it as the bad things that a few misguided, sinful individuals perpetrate. But it becomes a far more complex issue when those anxieties that arise from the basic contradictions and ambiguities that are integral to our humanness become incorporated into the very fabric of our community life. The evil that is always threatening to undo the civility of society is all the harder to recognize and to confront when it is hidden within the relatively benign practices and attitudes of a whole culture. It becomes very easy for me to deny that I am a racist when that word is defined for me by Klansmen and church bombers and ranting segregationists. But my complacency becomes a bit harder to defend when I am asked why there are no black families living in my neighborhood...why fifty years after the civil rights movement began, the city of Nashville is still largely a segregated community...why my tax-supported public schools are failing so miserably to educate young African-Americans...why I sent my younger daughter to a private school...why the medical care that I take for granted is denied to so many poor people of color...why I have such a hard time acknowledging that my financial and economic success, my status in the community, did not—as I would like to think—come about merely because I was smart and worked hard, but also because I was blessed from the beginning with a "white man's head start." The simplistic way in which our Western "Christian" culture has taught us to think about evil, in terms of the sins of individual persons, has not only tended to load us down with misplaced feelings of guilt about our imperfections, but, ironically, it has also tended to let us off the hook when it comes to living as morally responsible individuals in an "infected" society.

There is a small church in my neighborhood that I pass often when I am out walking for exercise. It has a sign out front facing the street that announces the name of the congregation and its denomination and includes one of those slotted boards with moveable letters on which various announcements and messages can be spelled out. For more than a year (at the time of this writing) the headline message on the board has remained the same: "Be imitators of God. Eph. 5:1." Every time I walk by that sign I find myself wondering about the implications of that exhortation. I wonder if that is what the minister of that church really wants the members of his congregation to be. Be imitators of God? Isn't that really the problem? Isn't that precisely the "temptation" that, according to the mythmakers of Genesis, the subtle serpent employed in the seduction of our first parents: "If you eat this fruit, you will be like God"? And haven't we been falling for that temptation ever since? Isn't that precisely the game we *Homo sapiens* have been playing at ever since we crossed the bridge out of Eden into the ambiguous contradictions of our humanness? There is a great opposition warring between our "angel" and our "animal" selves. It makes us very uncomfortable being neither this nor that, and all we want is to feel good about ourselves. So, with all the subtle variations that human genius can devise, we are constantly reinventing the old children's game of King on the Mountain. If we can't really be like God, at least we can be more like Him than the next guy. If we cannot really achieve immortality, we can perhaps feel immortal by being the strongest or the richest or the most powerful or the prettiest or the purest or the most famous or the most beloved or the ones with the smartest, most successful children, etc, etc, etc…Of course, some efforts to overcome the natural contradictions by imitating God are more obvious than others. The racist, in his belief that his skin color makes him superior, is an imitator of God. The Nazis, with their notions of a master race, were imitators of God. The exploiter of the environment for profit and power exercises his dominion over the world as an imitator of God.

But that strategy for dealing with our humanness never works. We can never be good enough, rich enough, smart enough, popular enough, powerful enough (enough like God?), to get rid of our limitations and contradictions. We can never be good enough to get back into the garden. The garden of paradise is not for humans anyway; evolution has equipped us to live in a community far more interesting and exciting than a boring Eden. The only paradise we will ever have is the one we build on earth, and it will be as contradictory and as problematical and as imperfect as we are, but it will be far more interesting and a whole lot more enjoyable than that freedomless, choiceless, old heavenly garden that we in the West have been taught to believe is our reward for being good. All that pretentious effort to be good and powerful and right and deserving and the best of whatever is the source of most of our problems anyway. A human animal is all I am ever going to be, so I need to stop fighting it and relax into my humanity. After all is said and done, isn't the ultimate sin (pardon my final use of that awful word) the rejection of the gift of the freedom and responsibility that came with our evolution into *Homo sapiens?* So, what is required of me is simply to accept the gift of my humanness, with all its lumps and limitations, embarrassing animal necessities and stumbling imperfections, ambiguities and contradictions, and, yes, its inevitable end. And when I am tempted to start impressing someone by pretending to be more and better than I am, I just need to learn to forgive myself for that stumble, pick myself up, brush away my silly pretensions, and start all over again being who I really am.

I know that I will find this life so much more enjoyable, and I will find myself once again free to dream dreams and to climb the spiritual heights to which only humans can aspire, and I will hurt a whole lot fewer people in the process.

TELL ME A NEW STORY

And don't leave anything out

I HAVE A CONFESSION TO MAKE. It has to do with how I became a Presbyterian minister. More precisely, it has to do with how I managed to pass the examination for ordination into the ministry. It so happened that during the exam, when I was being interrogated about my personal religious beliefs, I didn't exactly tell "the whole truth and nothing but the truth." In fact, to be perfectly honest (after almost fifty years), on one particular point, "before God and a church full of witnesses," I simply lied to the questioner.

Now, before I am convicted in the reader's mind of a heinous breach of ethical standards and labeled a complete charlatan, allow me, in my defense, to describe the circumstances, which I hope may mitigate somewhat the seriousness of my crime. For that purpose it will help, I believe, to have some background on how the ordination of ministers was handled in the Presbyterian Church at that time. When a young man decided that he would like—or more piously, that he was called—to be a minister (in my day, the ordination of women had not yet been approved), it was standard procedure for him to apply for candidacy to the Presbytery of which his local church was a member. (The Presbytery was a representative governing body made up of delegates from all of the congregations in a given geographical area, in this case the Birmingham Presbytery, to which my local church belonged. The delegates always included at least one lay elder, called a ruling elder, and the minister or ministers, called teaching elders, from each of its member congregations. The name, Presbyterian, indeed, denotes a church governed by elders, from the word for elder, *presbuteros* in New Testament Greek.) The applicant would be questioned—usually rather cursorily at this point—about his religious experience and his calling, and when he had satisfied those august "fathers and brethren" about his sincerity and dedication, he would be officially "taken under the care of Presbytery" as a candidate for the ministry. That meant that the Presbytery now had the official responsibility for overseeing his preparation for ordination. In actual practice, the educational requirements for the ministry had been pretty much standardized by the denomination many years earlier. A person desiring to become a Presbyterian minister must have had a four year college degree before entering an approved theological seminary, or divinity school, for an additional three-year curriculum that included the study of the Old and New Testaments in their original languages of Hebrew and Greek, as well as basic and advanced courses in theology and Presbyterian doctrine, church history, apologetics (defending the faith), homiletics (the art of preaching), pastoral care, etc., all the areas in which a parish minister would need to be well grounded. Upon graduation from the seminary and upon receiving a call to serve as a minister or assistant minister of a church congregation, he must appear before the Presbytery (and this was critical in my case) of *the church to which he was newly called.* There he would undergo a rigorous interrogation on subjects ranging from his knowledge of the Bible and church doctrine to his personal religious experience and his adherence to orthodox Presbyterian belief. The formal part of the examination was conducted by the members of a special commission appointed by the Presbytery for this purpose, but when that was concluded, the floor would be opened for any delegate to raise any question that might be on his mind regarding the candidate's knowledge, his piety, or his orthodoxy.

By the time I came up for my ordination exam, I was about as well prepared as formal training could afford. I held a degree in English (with some elective courses in Bible) from Presbyterian College in Clinton, South Carolina, and had graduated with honors from Columbia Theological Seminary in Decatur, Georgia, with major emphases in Hebrew and pastoral psychology. In addition to the standard three-year course, I had spent a twelve-month internship between my middle and senior year as the student pastor of a small congregation in the mountain community of Bethel, near Canton, North Carolina. And during the summer before returning to the seminary for my final year, I had undertaken an intensive ten-week course in Clinical Pastoral Education at Elgin State Hospital in Elgin, Illinois, a program designed to hone one's skills as a pastoral caregiver in the challenging setting of a hospital for the emotionally disturbed. Based upon those credentials there would seem to be no obvious reason why I should have been the least bit worried about my upcoming examination. But I was.

The problem was *where* the examination was to take place. As I described earlier, my first parish as an ordained minister was in Summerton, South Carolina, and the Summerton Presbyterian Church was a member of Harmony Presbytery (interesting name, given the times) whose boundaries encompassed several of the most socially and religiously conservative counties in a very socially and religiously conservative state. And, as I also noted, these were tumultuous and difficult days of change in the South. I could just imagine some old elder—bless his heart—who was anxious to the core about all this stuff going on and mad as hell at what all those liberal outsiders were coming in and doing to his once comfortable way of life, just lying in wait, his proverbial guns loaded, to take out his frustrations on this young city boy with all his degrees and his hifalutin education: "Who needs all those foreign languages and those 'revised versions' of the Bible? What we need is some old-time religion. If the King James Version was good enough for Jesus, it oughta be good enough for anybody...and all those notions about that pastoral psychology stuff and something called 'Biblical criticism'! You aren't supposed to criticize the Bible; you're just supposed to believe it...and there's no tellin' what other kind of radical ideas he may have caught from all those seminary professors!" (Although Columbia Seminary had the reputation of being the most conservative of our theological schools, some new light *had* begun to brighten its halls.) It was that old elder from some rural church in Harmony Presbytery—admittedly a figment of my anxious imagination, but not so far-fetched as it turned out— about whom I was worrying as the trial that would literally determine my future approached. And, though he may not have been exactly the person I imagined, he *was* there.

Harmony Presbytery met that June of 1958 at the Hebron Presbyterian Church in the town of Wedgefield, South Carolina. Though it appears as a small dot on the state highway maps, Wedgefield, as I remember it, hardly qualified as a town at all, boasting no commercial establishments other than a service station or two and no governmental buildings other than the volunteer fire department, though there must have been a county school in the area. It was located on State Road 261, about four miles in distance, but a whole lot further in time, off of the modern four-lane highway that runs between the state capitol of Columbia and the county seat of Sumter. At mid-century it appeared to be a loosely concentrated gathering of homes ranging in permanence and dignity from a few mobile homes whose owners most likely commuted to work in nearby towns to a scattering of impressive brick residences suggesting that there might still be some local heirs of the large cotton plantations that once flourished on the sandy bluffs just east of the great Santee Swamp. While some cotton was still grown in the area, it was quickly being replaced by less labor-intensive crops, the principle one around Wedgefield seeming to be pine trees for pulpwood. Immediately south of the community lay the Manchester State Forest, a huge unpopulated expanse of cultivated pines, large enough to contain a gunnery and bombing range used for practice by the planes of Shaw Air Force Base in Sumter and by the fighter squadron of the South Carolina Air National Guard in Columbia.

As well as serving as the social and spiritual hub of Wedgefield, the tiny Presbyterian Church shone like an architectural jewel at the center of a scattered surrounding of rather plain and uninteresting edifices. It was set back about two hundred yards from the main road in a grove of pine and Spanish moss draped live oaks. I don't know if it was a survivor of the ravages of Civil War or was of more recent construction, but it had about it the air of an old citizen who is quite comfortably mature and well settled in his place. It was of wood construction on a foundation of what appeared to be handmade brick, a basically square building with a modest but perfectly proportioned steeple offset to one corner. Painted gleaming white overall, it stood in brilliant contrast to its backdrop of pines and oaks, while its dark green trim seemed to provide an organic connection to its natural environment. Its picturesque postcard perfection and its peacefully quiet setting did not in any way recommend the little church as a theater for the controversy and confrontation I was anticipating.

Promptly at 10:00 a.m. the June meeting of Harmony Presbytery was called to order by its moderator, and, after prayers for divine guidance and the reading of the minutes of the previous session, it took up its agenda of old business with the reporting of committees, motions to adopt committee recommendations, seconds to the motions, discussion, and votes to adopt, to amend, to table for future consideration, or to reject. There is perhaps no deliberative body in the world as proficient in carrying out business "with decency and in good order" as an official convening of Presbyterian elders when they are faithfully working under the rules of the Presbyterian *Book of Church Order* (that book probably ranks second in esteem among traditional Presbyterians only to the Bible itself, and, after attending a few Presbytery meetings, one might begin to wonder which book is really "on first"). And these elders proved no exception to the Presbyterian love of order and efficient deliberation. By the noon hour, most of the routine business had been neatly dispatched and the meeting recessed for a traditional country church dinner-on-the-grounds lunch hosted by the women of the church. After a sumptuous meal the Presbytery reconvened for the consideration of new business. The main order of that new business was *me*, plus one other candidate whose father was the pastor of the Wedgefield Church and who had been given special dispensation to be examined in his home church because he was not going directly into a parish but to further graduate study. He was already known personally by many of the elders there, so, as it turned out, I was the only real newcomer under consideration.

The examination was thorough, with various members of the commission assigned to question the two of us alternately on our Christian experience ("I don't remember a time when I was not a Christian," seemed a natural response from one who had been baptized in infancy), our calling to the ministry ("It was not so much a sudden revelation as it was a gradual sense that grew over many years that this was the vocation to which God was calling me…"). The questions having to do specifically with our knowledge of the Bible and doctrinal matters posed no real problem for either of us. While it is always stressful to have to speak off-the-cuff in response to unanticipated queries for which one has no way of preparing in advance—especially when so much is riding on the answers—we did hold the advantage of having only recently left the classroom and whatever knowledge we had was at least fresh in our minds. So, I was beginning to feel, with great relief, that I had cleared the major hurdle when the chairman asked if any of the commission members had any further questions, and there being none, announced, "We are now open for questions from the floor." That is when my "old elder" who had previously existed only in my nervous imagination took on flesh and blood, stood up, and looked directly at me.

"Mr. DuBose," he intoned with a solemn furrowing of his brow, "I have just one question I would like to put to you, sir: Do you believe in the Virgin Birth of Jesus as a literal historical fact, and do you hold that belief to be central to your faith in Jesus Christ as your personal savior?" ("Sir, I believe that was two questions," my nonexistent defense attorney might have objected.)

We have all heard stories of persons whose whole lives seemed to flash before their eyes in moments of extreme crisis or dire threat. I can't say that my whole twenty-six years passed before me in the seconds following that question, but certainly the last eight or so that I had spent preparing for my chosen career seemed to be hanging out there rather limply on the line, and I could see the future I had dreamed spiraling down into a dark sinkhole. This was the question I had feared the most and the way it was posed allowed for no equivocation. I was convinced that if I could not answer it to his satisfaction, then my "old elder" would probably be joined by many of his like-minded confederates, a likely majority of the presbyters, in righteously clamoring for my rejection as a candidate for the ministry.

Like most Westerners who had come from religious families and had grown up in the Church, I had simply accepted the whole Christmas narrative as true. The story of Mary and Joseph traveling to Bethlehem and having to stay in a stable when there was no room in the inn, the angels appearing to the shepherds, the three wise men coming from the east, all were part of the story of the birth of God's son that was told and retold every December, the very best part of the year for children. Knowing that story and hearing it read over and over and sung about in favorite carols, and seeing it acted out in annual pageants was just part of the culture into which I had been born. I don't ever recall from Sunday school days any particular attention being paid to, or questions being raised about, how a young woman who was a virgin (a what?) could have a baby. That just wasn't discussed. As a youngster I didn't really understand the "virgin" part of the great carol *Silent Night, Holy Night* any more than I understood the "round yon" part. You know, "...round yon virgin, mother and child." And when the

Bible said that Mary was "great with child" I probably just assumed that it meant that she was "good with children," or something like that. We didn't concern ourselves with the details of the story; we simply took it at face value as part of the wonderful mystery of Christmas, which was one chapter in the Bible story of God's creation of the world and of His love for His chosen children and his sacrifice of his own son for their salvation, the story that told us who we were and how we ought to live.

When I got older and was a bit more informed biologically, it might have seemed something of a stretch to think of a young woman getting pregnant without the benefit of sexual intercourse with a very human male, but somehow that scientific knowledge still did not impinge upon the truth of the Christmas miracle. The scientific and the religious were still two separate worlds. I was, however, becoming aware that some "modern thinkers" were questioning the veracity of the Bible's miracle stories and that the "virgin birth" story seemed to be a main target of their skepticism. I also came across the fact that other religions, even more ancient than Christianity, had, as part of their mythologies, stories of gods being born of virgins. The Christian creeds were not unique in that sense. But still I wasn't ready to give up what had always been a primary declaration of orthodox Christian belief. It was, ironically, not until I got to the seminary and began to learn more about how the biblical text came into being and to read some of it in its original languages that my naive acceptance of the literal truth of the virgin birth of Jesus simply fell apart.

I learned, for instance, that the verse in Matthew that

is translated into English as, "Behold a virgin shall conceive and bear a son; and his name shall be called Emmanuel, God with us" (Matthew 1:23,KJV), which is a quote from the book of Isaiah (Isaiah 7:14), is actually a mistranslation—or at least a very "loose" translation—from the Old Testament Hebrew. The word in the Old Testament that is translated into both Greek and English (King James Version) as "virgin" does not clearly mean that. The Hebrew word means literally "young woman." I suppose that one could have made the assumption that a "young woman" is also a "virgin" (not any more certainly), but Isaiah does not say that specifically. And to say "...a young woman shall conceive and bear a son..." is to say something quite different than "...a virgin shall conceive..." (In the Revised Standard Version of the Bible that error is corrected in its translation of Isaiah.) What was going on here? Was this simply a mistake on the part of an early translator of Isaiah into Greek? Even if it was an honest error, the discrepancy still appeared to undercut the authority of the Old Testament prophecy, which Christians had always relied upon to undergird their belief in the virgin birth. I came to believe, however, that it was more than a simple error. We know that the four Gospels are not simple narratives of the life of Jesus written down by the four authors whose names they bear. They are each, more or less, a pastiche of various materials, from oral as well as written sources, put together by unknown persons a good many years after the death of Jesus, when the early church felt the need to have a written record of his life. We know also that the Gospels are not straightforward reports of his life, but inevitably reflect the particular biases of their individual composers. They each have a different slant on the story. I gradually came to believe that the composer (or composer*s*) of the book of Matthew had intentionally skewed the translation, or at the very least rationalized a "loose" interpretation of the Hebrew "young woman" in Isaiah to read "virgin" in order to provide written authority for the early Church's developing doctrine of the divinity of Jesus. According to my understanding of how the Gospel narratives had been put together, I could see that the notion that Jesus had been born of a virgin was quite possibly an invention by the Church, introduced long after the fact, for the purposes of strengthening its own theological position. I could no longer believe that Jesus was actually born of a virgin, any more than I was, but at that point, I also didn't believe that dropping that one part of the traditional story made any difference at all to my religious faith. I just couldn't see that belief in the virgin birth added anything essential to my Christianity.

Now, is there anyone who could possibly imagine that my "old elder" would have appreciated an attempt on my part to educate him regarding these fine points of biblical interpretation, or that he would have thanked me kindly for liberating him from his slavish adherence to a belief in the virgin birth as an historical fact? I don't think so. And what was I to do? I had dedicated my life to the ministry; I had spent all those years getting trained for it; I had already accepted a call to the Summerton church; Rebecca and I were to be married in a couple of weeks, and the church had already completely redecorated the manse in anticipation of the newlyweds moving in. I was not prepared for any other kind of work, I had no money for further schooling, and after being rejected by one Presbytery, I wasn't likely to get another offer. I saw all of this with total clarity in the seconds after that question was put to me. So, I took the only path I saw as reasonably available. With hardly a moment's hesitation, I looked my interrogator straight in the face and lied: "Yes, sir, I do so believe."

I can honestly say that my internal "moral seismograph" hardly twitched as I spoke those words. Nor did I flinch, expecting an imminent lightning strike on the steeple of that pretty little church. I don't recall feeling the slightest hint of guilt over my deliberately false statement. Considering that I had always been a basically honest person, and that what I had just done, given the sacred setting, might be considered a more serious form of perjury than even a false testimony in a court of law, it is perhaps surprising that I could have excused myself so easily for that calculated deception. Maybe I was just rationalizing that I could affirm my belief in the virgin birth as a kind of symbolic statement, that it was just a kind of metaphor for the goodness and purity of Jesus that didn't have to be taken literally? But the precise way in which the question had been put would seem to rule that out. My interrogator was completely clear about what he was asking me to affirm. And I knew that my response was a lie. But I believed at the time that telling that lie was a necessary and therefore acceptable thing to do on two accounts. First, I didn't think that there was anything to be gained—and there was a terrible lot to be lost—by engaging in a debate on the floor of Presbytery with one reactionary old elder over the literal interpretation of the Bible. I certainly wasn't going to change his mind, and all I would accomplish by giving him the benefit of my enlightened thinking would be to scuttle my own career. And I had made too great an investment in my future to allow that to happen at this late date. Second, I really didn't think the question was important, anyway. I thought *he* was the one who was in the wrong to ask such a question in the first place. What did it really matter, in the big picture of things, whether or not I believed in the virgin birth? Why get hung up on that one insignificant part of the larger story that forms the basis of the Christian religion? It wasn't hard to dismiss rather cavalierly a question I thought was basically silly and of no consequence.

I have had reason over the years to question both of my rationalizations of what I did that day. On the first count I have wondered, given the path my ministerial career ultimately took, whether I might not have saved myself a lot of grief (as well as preserving my basic integrity) by simply telling the truth and letting the cards fall out how they may. But then, as we know, hindsight is 20/20, and I am not at all sure, given the predicament in which I found myself back then, that I would respond differently if the situation repeated itself. I'll let the reader decide whether my prevarication was forgivable under the circumstances. On the second count, however, I have decided that I was dead wrong. I have, indeed, concluded that the question at issue was not as insignificant, nor as petty, as I had originally deemed it to be. In fact, I have come to believe that my old elder's query, however reactionary and overly simplistic, was the expression of a legitimate concern over what was happening to Christianity in mid-twentieth-century America. I think that what was worrying him was not just the orthodoxy of one young seminary graduate regarding the one specific question of the virgin birth. That was only the symptom of a general anxiety, which he may or may not have been able to articulate even to himself, but which he must have felt very deeply—a concern over the erosion of respect in our culture for the whole biblical story that forms the basis of the Christian religion. I believe that he saw, much more clearly than I did, that once we start to pick apart the story on which the faith is based, deciding for ourselves which parts of it are credible and which are not, we have started down a slippery slope toward a more general unbelief. He was right, I now believe, and while my deceptive answer to his question may have laid *his* worries about me and my belief to rest, I should have been warned—had I fully grasped the implications of what I had just done—that I was daringly close to stepping over the crest of a precipitous sliding board into a more thorough skepticism. But that concern was not uppermost in my mind at the moment. All I could think about right then was saving my young career, which I had done (at least temporarily). I passed the exam and was approved for ordination by a unanimous vote of the elders of Harmony Presbytery.

I spent ten years in the Presbyterian ministry, and during that time, in spite of that brief moment of dishonesty with which it began, and in spite of my growing doubt about some facets of the biblical story, I was neither a pretender nor a charlatan. I sincerely believed in what I was trying to be and do and say. I believed in the Church into which I had been born and which had nurtured me in the faith. I believed in the Church, not as a select society for the godly and the righteous few, but as an open community of people whose only distinction was their acceptance of the unconditional love of God as witnessed in the life and teachings of Jesus. I believed that the Church had a mission, not only in response to the spiritual yearnings of individual believers, but also to be about the wider work of building a just and equitable society. As a Presbyterian teaching elder, I believed that it was my task to offer to my congregation an interpretation of the New Testament teachings and the historic doctrines of the Church that was intelligent and fresh and vitally relevant to the lives of contemporary men and women. That responsibility I took very seriously.

At the same time, however, my skepticism continued to grow. Most of my questions and doubts, I now realize, had to do with what might be called the supernatural parts of the Christian story. I had trouble with virgin births and miracles and other such divine contraventions of the natural order of things. The mythology of the Old Testament didn't present me with too much of a problem. Early on in my seminary studies, I read the Genesis saga of the six-day creation of the universe in its original Hebrew and was convinced that it was essentially a wonderful example of ancient poetry that was never meant to be taken literally. Stories such as the "Tower of Babel," "Noah's Ark," and the "Parting of the Red Sea" were plainly folkloric tales invented by a pre-scientific people for purposes of illustrating certain moral or religious lessons (the geological impossibility of a flood that could cover the entire earth, not to speak of the logistical and sanitary nightmare of bringing all of those animals on board one big wooden boat to float around on an endless ocean for five or six months, makes the notion of a literal reading of such tales merely ludicrous).

The New Testament, however, posed an entirely different problem. How was I to deal with stories of Jesus' miracles, which were purported to be the eyewitness accounts of persons who were present when those miracles occurred? The fact that there could have been no witnesses to the insemination of the Virgin Mary by the Holy Spirit made that somewhat easier to dismiss as a sincere but mistaken attempt on the part of the early Church fathers to undergird the believers' faith in the divinity of Jesus. But the miracles attributed to Jesus himself were a different matter; the story claims that there were witnesses. It was tempting to apply to the accounts of his healing of the lame and blind and his "casting out of demons" what I had learned while working in a mental hospital about psychiatric disorders and psychosomatic cures, but that kind of modern rationalization seemed to be little more than a cop-out on my part simply to avoid the real problem posed by the miracle stories. Besides, it said nothing about the Gospel writers' descriptions of his extraordinary ability to walk on water, to bring back a man from the dead, to change water into wine, and to feed four thousand people to full satisfaction on rations consisting of seven loaves and a few fishes. Did these disruptions in the natural order of things actually occur as they were reported? Or, were such stories merely the expressions of enthusiastic hyperbole on the part of his disciples? Or, as I had concluded in the case of the virgin birth, were such stories later inventions on the part of Church leaders that were added to the narrative to strengthen acceptance of the idea that Jesus was the true Son of God? And if that was the case, then just how much of the purported eyewitness account can be discredited in this manner before the whole story begins to fall apart? (My old elder's concern again?) It was a long time before I was ready to face the implications of that question, and for most of my time in the ministry, I dealt with my problem with the miracles of Jesus by not dealing with them at all. For the most part I simply ignored them, choosing in my teaching and preaching to focus instead on what the New Testament has to say about being human, about loving and caring for each other, about forgiving and being forgiven, about living free of fear and guilt.

Then there was that other miracle—the big one—the one which, if a person truly professes to be a Christian, will be pretty difficult, if not impossible, simply to ignore. Did I really believe, as I said over and over again in reciting the Apostles' Creed, that Jesus "...was crucified, dead and buried..." and that on *"the third day he rose again from the dead; He ascended into Heaven..."* and so on? Did I actually believe that a man could die—really die—be sealed in a tomb for three days, and then get up out of that grave—after some angels moved the stone that blocked the entrance—once more a walking, talking, flesh-and-blood, living person? And what about the business of his physical ascension directly into heaven? If he ascended bodily to heaven, then heaven must be a physical place somewhere. And where in the universe could that place be? I suppose that, as a young person, I had once again merely accepted these parts of the story as I had accepted all the rest of it. It was just part of being a Christian. And I certainly could not have gotten through ten Easter seasons as an ordained clergyman without acknowledging a belief of some kind in the empty tomb, whatever questions were beginning to eat at that belief. My records show that I preached about the resurrection on those special Sundays, though I don't recall anything of what I actually said. I know that I never reached the point of openly admitting, to myself or to anyone else, that I just didn't believe that anymore, but I am also sure that, by the time I called it quits as a minister, that critical element of the Christian creed had pretty much lost its credibility for me.

Perhaps surprisingly, I did not leave the ministry solely because of my growing skepticism. There were other, more practical reasons for that decision. One was my continuing disillusionment over the Church's intransigence in responding to the civil rights revolution and my despair that it could ever be the redemptive agent in society that I had believed it was called to be. Then there was my increasing awareness that I just didn't enjoy being a minister. I just wasn't comfortable in that role. I didn't have the people skills to be a good pastor—a large part of the job—and I had none of the administrative skills that a large church required of its staff members. As a minister, all I wanted to be was a theologian and a preacher, and that was not enough. In the final analysis, though, I gave up the robes and the backward collar largely because, for all my life, I had really wanted to be an artist. I had been drawing since I was old enough to hold a pencil (my first "published" work of art was a drawing I did for the school newspaper when I was a first grader!). As a teenager I had taught myself to paint in oils and in watercolors. When, during my high school years, the city of Birmingham opened its first art museum with a donation of paintings from the Kress Foundation, I was one of its most avid visitors. How many Sunday afternoons did I spend poring over those Renaissance panels, the first "real" art I had ever seen "in the flesh"! The small church college I attended had no art department, but for three years, I was the college yearbook's art editor and cover designer. That talent and my persistent interest in the visual arts, however, had brought me little encouragement at home. I think my mother probably looked upon it as a nice hobby; my father just thought I was strange. Once, when the CEO of his company was visiting from New York and came to dinner in our home, he saw some of my amateur artwork and made the audacious suggestion that he might be willing to help me go to art school. It appeared, from the silence that followed his proposal, that I was the only one who had actually heard what he said. There was never a single mention of his offer from my parents. As far as they were concerned, he might have as well have been suggesting "a trip to the moon on gossamer wings." Art school? What a strange notion! They already knew what I was going to do and what I was going to be. And so, because of the pressure of family assumptions and the sheer weight of my religious upbringing (I may have been baptized by "sprinkling," but as far as my religious involvement was concerned, it was "total immersion"), I had made my commitment to the Church, and had almost missed my other calling.

When my father put his big question to me, "Have you lost your faith?" I wasn't prepared to give him the simple answer that his apparently straightforward query seemed to require. And I don't think that was what he wanted anyway. He was looking for an explanation. He wanted to know what had happened to change me so completely. He didn't understand anything about art or what it meant to be an artist, and I had never discussed with him the difficulties I had experienced being a minister. So he was completely unprepared for my sudden abandonment of the calling that *he* knew I was meant for. He probably could not have been more mystified had I changed my gender or the color of my skin. It was as if the person he had known and been proud to call his son (not that he ever told me that to my face) had turned out to be some strange creature he didn't recognize (the chin whiskers I had grown didn't help!). How could this have happened? I wasn't ready to give him an explanation; I hadn't even started to sort out the "theological" reasons for my sudden change of direction for myself. Those factors had sort of gotten covered up by the more immediate causes that I mentioned above. And I had been too busy making up for lost time in my formal art education to give much thought to the old questions and doubts that had dogged me as a clergyman. It would be many years before I would pick up those questions again, like a cold case forensics detective going over the old wreckage of my former career to determine once and for all what had caused it to crash. It would be thirty years after his death before I returned to the "faith" of my father's question for a post-mortem on the religion that had totally dominated the first half of my life. It would be at least that long before I began to realize that what had happened to me was exactly what that old elder in South Carolina had feared back in 1958. And it all had to do with the story upon which my Christian faith had been based and what happens when that story begins to lose its credibility.

Human beings are storytelling animals. That is one of the more significant attributes by which we can distinguish ourselves from our closest animal cousins: we tell stories; they don't. I suspect that our earliest ancestors started making up stories pretty soon after they had crossed the evolutionary bridge into *Homo sapienism* and began to feel the need to explain themselves to themselves and to each other. It was one of the main ways they found to make sense of their new experience of being human. The practice had probably begun even before the domestication of fire, but that surely must have stimulated the development of this new art— something to do on those long nights while they huddled around the fire keeping themselves warm. Storytelling might even be considered the mother of all the art forms that now grace our humanity. Could not painting and sculpture, music and dance, certainly theater and literature, be seen as extensions and refinements of that original sense-making activity? And if we understand that the making up of stories was one of the first ways early people attempted to explain the workings of the natural world, we might even conclude that that simple activity was the fountainhead of modern science. Certainly it was essential to the birth of religion as a human activity.

One of the best general descriptions of religion I have ever come across was put forward, ironically, not by a theologian or a philosopher, but by a scientist, the physicist and astronomer Chet Raymo: "A vital religious faith has three components: *a shared cosmology (a story of the universe and our place in it)* [italics mine], spirituality (personal response to the mystery of the world), and liturgy (public expressions of awe and gratitude, including rites of passage)."[1] At the heart of every religion, almost without exception, is a story that is believed by its adherents to answer certain basic human questions: Who am I? Where did I come from? Why am I here? What happens to me when I die? Most religious stories also include a creation myth, a story of how the world as we know it came to be. And Christianity is no exception. Christianity, like its mother faith, Judaism, is supremely a "storybook" religion. That is one of its main strengths: that it tells a vivid, compelling and memorable story. Listening to stories is how most of us learned what it means to be Christian or Jewish. What I remember from my childhood religious education is not the catechism that I was coerced to memorize in its entirety, with its questions and answers about Christian doctrine: "Question: Who made you? Answer: God made me. Question: What else did God make? Answer: God made all things." That's all I can remember of the catechism. But I could tell you some stories! Beginning with "In the beginning," and the six-day saga of creation, stories of Adam and Eve in the garden, of the temptation by the serpent, of Cain and Abel, of the Tower of Babel, of Noah and the Ark, of Abraham and Isaac, of Joseph and his coat of many colors, of Moses as a baby found in the bulrushes by the Pharaohs daughter, of God speaking to him out of the burning bush, of the Passover and the exodus out of Egypt and the parting of the Red Sea, of the giving of the Ten Commandments on Mt. Sinai, of the Children of Israel wandering in search of the Promised Land, of David and Goliath, of David the King and his sin with Bathsheba (now that's a spicy story!), and of the wisdom of Solomon. And then there are the New Testament stories of Mary and Joseph and the baby Jesus born in Bethlehem, of the shepherds and the angels and the three Wise Men, of King Herod and the slaughter of the innocents, of Jesus' teachings and his own stories called parables, of the Sermon on the Mount, of his miracles—the loaves and fishes, raising Lazarus from the dead, turning water into wine—of the Last Supper, his betrayal by Judas, his arrest, his trial, his crucifixion, and of the empty tomb and his appearance to his disciples…

So many good stories! Stories that captured the imagination of the whole Western world and became the inspiration for some of its greatest music, art, and literature. Stories that, in summary, add up to this: There is this supernatural being whose existence is distinct from own and our world's existence who is called God, who is a person, a mind, a "spiritual being," who is all-powerful and all-knowing, and who, of his own will, created the universe and all of its inhabitants, who made the earth and gave it to his human family for them to rule over and enjoy. Throughout history He has continually acted on behalf of His people, watching over them and personally directing the affairs of the world, attending to the daily lives of even the least of his creatures. He made us, and when we die, if we have lived according to his commandments, we will go to a place called heaven to live with Him forever. Amen. This story, along with its illustrative parts, was the core narrative that, despite an ever-present counterculture of doubt and unbelief, nevertheless informed Western civilization for almost two millennia as to how the world came to be, who we humans are, and where we are going. This has been our culture-shaping mythology, our "shared cosmology," our "story of the universe and our place in it." And this was my story for a good part of my life…until the persistence of nagging questions began to erode its hold on me.

In an earlier chapter, in a discussion of spirituality and its relationship to organized religion, I suggested that the difference between the two has to do with the difference between questions and answers. Spirituality has to do with questions— the searching questions of the individual in response to the mystery of life; whereas religion has to do with answers, usually in the form of the "truths" agreed upon by a consensus of believers, answers handed down from one generation to the next. Those formulated answers to the big questions make up the shared story that informs and unites religious communities and sometime even whole cultures. When I left the Church, it was partly because of my growing skepticism with regard to the answers the Church had told me were the truth about life, as well as my growing disillusionment with the whole story that forms the basis of the Christian religion. It was only after many years—when I had finally dropped the habit of looking at the world through "stained glass windows" and was totally engrossed in the secular world of art and academia—that I discovered that, while I might have put down the answers that I had been given, the questions, which were my personal response to the world around me, remained. And I realized that what had happened to me—and what happens, I believe, to many people who, like me, were born into religious families, religious institutions, and religious cultures—was that I learned the answers before I ever knew what the questions were. And I concluded that that is what traditional religion too often does for its adherents: it puts the cart before the horse. It supplies answers for questions the believer has never learned to ask, with the result that religion loses its vital connection to life as it is really lived and becomes for many merely a cultural habit.

Now that I had turned away from simply accepting the ready-made answers of my childhood faith, I had begun to find my own questions. But I was like the young man I came across recently in a book titled *Eat, Pray, Love* by Elizabeth Gilbert. She describes him as a friend who found himself in a deep spiritual and emotional crisis brought on by the birth of his first child right on the heels of the death of his mother to whom he had been very close. He longed again for a sacred place where he could go, a ritual he could perform that might bring him consolation and healing and help him sort out his contradictory feelings of sorrow and joy. But he could not go back to the church of his childhood because, as he put it, "I can't buy it anymore...knowing what I know."[2]

I know what he was talking about. I, too, have found myself longing to be at home again in that familiar sacred place into which I was born and which gave me my identity and, for a while at least, a motivating mission in life. I've wished many times that I could go back there and find it as I left it. But I know I can't. I remember once going as a tourist into a fourteenth-century cathedral in Wales only to find my historical objectivity washed away by a flooding of tears in response to the booming chords of the cathedral's great pipe organ. I was embarrassed and confused to find myself weeping uncontrollably in that public place crowded with other tourists. Was this some sort of revelatory spiritual experience? I think not. I think it was more likely one of those powerful synesthetic moments, when an old familiar song or an intense forgotten odor can transport one back with extraordinary vividness to a time long past. In that moment I was back in Birmingham at the "Old First" Presbyterian Church, with its marvelous four-manual Aeolian-Skinner organ, where I first joined the adult choir as a teenager and began to sing the great choral music of the Christian tradition. These were tears of nostalgia, and of grief, for what could never be again. The intensity of my feelings was a measure of how important my early life in the Church had been for me. And I knew all of that was gone forever. I have attended the weddings of young couples happily in love and listened to them recite their vows and watched them as the minister or priest intoned his pious liturgical phrases about this "divinely sanctioned union" and wondered if the principle actors in this sacred drama, these two young people so thoroughly grounded in this high-tech century, had any idea what he was talking about, or if they really cared. And I was sad for them, and for me, at what was lost in this disjuncture between those archaic words and these young people's contemporary notions of what is meaningful. I was obliged recently, on the occasion of a family christening, to attend a Sunday morning service at a small Lutheran church in a nearby town. I went somewhat begrudgingly, having not attended church in over thirty years and expecting to have to endure a mostly negative experience. It turned out, to my surprise, not to be like that at all. The congregation was warm and welcoming. The building itself, a contemporary design with pews arranged in semicircular rows, encouraged a feeling of community and an enthusiastic participation in the service (unlike most Presbyterian churches I had known where the traditional design, with pews in straight rows, tended to turn the congregation into an audience of onlookers). The pastor was relaxed and managed to convey a friendly informality even though fully robed in ritual finery and adhering fairly strictly to standard liturgical conventions. His sermon was well spoken and intelligible, non-moralistic, and mercifully brief. All in all, I was having a good time being back in church. Then came the reciting of the creed, the saying aloud of the standard petitions for divine guidance and mercy, and finally the celebration of the sacrament of Holy Communion. And I was once again just a visitor, a guest, an outsider. I appreciated what that congregation of people was doing. I admired their enthusiasm and their sincerity. I found nothing hypocritical or self-righteous about their affirmations of faith. Nor did I feel any condescension toward them for what some might deem to be a naive embracing of unexamined dogma. I respected them for the integrity of their individual quests, but I couldn't go with them down that religious road. I had been there before, and I knew that this was not a path that I could walk any longer. *"I can't buy it anymore,"* the young man said.

And just what is it that *I* can and cannot "buy"? I can buy the part that Chet Raymo lists as the second component of a vital religious faith: "spirituality (personal response to the mystery of the world)." Except that, in importance and precedence, I would list spirituality as the *first* component, not the second, in any kind of human religious experience or expression. I can buy the kind of spirituality that I have attempted to define in previous chapters, the spirituality that is the unique expression of mammalian, time-and-flesh-bound creatures who also happen to be equipped with transcendent imaginations, the kind of spirituality that arises out of our genuine perplexity at the mystery and ambiguity of our self-conscious existence. I can buy the questions. What I cannot buy anymore is the story I was told in church that was supposed to answer the questions, the old-man-in-the-sky story, the God story of this supernatural being who lives in heaven somewhere, who supposedly made us as we are (In *His* own image? Or is He made in *ours?*) and gave

us the earth to live on and rule over. *"I can't buy it anymore…
knowing what I know."*

And what is it that I know that makes the old beloved
story no longer credible for me? I know that human beings
are not special creations. We did not come into the world just
as we are by the specific, deliberate act of some supernatural being. Ever since humans started asking questions about
their own and the world's existence, they have been coming
up with all sorts of god stories to explain things they didn't
understand: sun gods, animal gods, tree gods, the Greek gods
on Mount Olympus, supernatural anthropomorphic gods…
but we do not any longer need to posit a supernatural creator
in order to explain our existence. We know how our earliest
human ancestors came to be, and it wasn't in a single act of
creation. Whatever mysterious power we might imagine being behind it all, and whatever language we find to make that
power real to us, we know that neither we nor the earth and
all its other inhabitants just appeared on the scene one day (or
in six days?) "out of whole cloth"; we were not *made*, as the
old theologians were want to say, *ex nihilo*, out of nothing. Our
existence is the result of a physical/chemical process that has
been taking place for billions and billions of years, and that,
until relatively recently, we had not even begun to understand.
We now know that the earth as a planet was formed more than
four and a half billion years ago, a tiny little seed in a vastly
expanding universe, and that the first signs of life appeared
in the primordial seas that washed over the new planet about
half a billion years later (pretty quickly in geologic time!). And
we know that from that initial urgent spark, all life on earth

has evolved. As the philosopher Philip Kitcher recently put it very plainly, "There is just one tree of life. All the living things that have ever existed on our planet are linked by processes of 'descent with modification,' so that even the organisms that seem least similar—an eagle and a seaweed, say—are derived from a common ancestor that lived at some point in the remote past."[3] We also know that the process that resulted in the amazing diversity of life on earth is that which Charles Darwin first hypothesized, and then formulated on the basis of the evidence that he saw, as evolution by natural selection. And finally, we know that our species, *Homo sapiens*, came into being by that process of "descent with modification" out of a group of primate populations that lived between 700,000 and 125,000 years ago.[4] When I say that we *know* this, I mean simply that I accept as a given that the Darwinian model of life's evolution by natural selection is the explanation that best fits the massive amount of evidence now available to us regarding our origins. The reliability of his theory has been demonstrated both by the fossil record and, more recently, by the mapping of the human genome and by DNA comparisons with other species. No creditable evidence has ever been brought forward that would persuade an informed and intellectually objective person that Darwin was substantially wrong. Evolution is as much a fact as gravity, and to deny that fact at this point in time is to be guilty of an intellectual foolishness comparable to denying that the earth orbits the sun.

Earlier I suggested that what was really bothering the old elder who tried to pin me down with regard to my belief in the Virgin Birth was not just a concern for one twenty-six-year-old ministerial candidate's orthodoxy. Whether or not he could have stated it in this way, his real worry, I believe, was over a general loss of respect in our culture for the biblical story that is the source of the Christian religion. And he was right to be worried. My own growing skepticism, had I let him in on it, would have been proof enough for him that his anxiety was well founded. What he feared was already happening, and has continued to happen. There was nothing unique about my experience. Whether you choose to call it the loss of faith that my father asked about, or the death of the main metaphors of traditional religious language that I wrote about in the first chapter, or the failure of the old supernatural story to answer our fundamental questions, "knowing what we now know", it is a culture-wide phenomenon. The signs are all around us. Chet Raymo points to some of them: "Why then do we hanker for miracles, aliens, UFOs, bleeding statues, angels, apocalypse? (And worship 'iconic' celebrities?) Why are we so quick to hand over our reason to the channelers, gurus, astrologers, faith healers, and promisers of a quick immortal fix (and I would add televangelists, reactionary fundamentalists, mega-church impresarios…)?" And he answers his own question, "Because we have lost our sense of a community story, a story of who we are, where we came from, where we're going. The old story still holds our attention, but it is a hollow shell. The New Story waits in the wings."[5]

For an increasing number of people today the "old story" has indeed become an empty shell, with its dependence on a literal belief in the existence of this supernatural anthropomorphic god-person who, we are told, made us and everything else by the mere imposition of his all-powerful will, who personally intervenes to help us out of the tight places of life, and who even rescues us from death itself. And if that story doesn't work for us any longer, where will we find a new one? We will forge it ourselves, just as all the old stories, including our Judeo-Christian story, were forged by our predecessors to answer the basic questions with which our humanity confronts us—Who are we? Where did we come from? Where are we going?—using as the material for our new story what we now know and are still learning about our origins and our place in the universe. In the first volume of *A History of the English-speaking Peoples*, Winston Churchill describes the success of the Roman Empire in imposing its *Pax Romana* on practically the entire Western world. It was a peace based upon the toleration of all religions under the umbrella of a "universal system of government." While it worked it was a remarkable achievement, but trouble was coming: "Every generation after the middle of the second century saw an increasing weakening of the system and a gathering movement towards a uniform religion. Christianity asked again all the questions which the Roman world deemed answered forever, and some that it had never thought of."[6] I believe that is exactly what is happening today. We are asking, again, all the questions that the *Christian* world deemed answered forever, *and some it has never thought of.* Chet Raymo goes on to point out that the scientists who have given us the knowledge "never thought of" by the authors of the Christian story, and the public information that will serve as the source material for the "New Story" have done a poor job of telling *their* story, but, he adds, "Perhaps it is not their task to be storytellers. The skills required for scientific discovery are not the skills of narration."[7] The scientists and technologists will not write the new story; that is not their job, nor will the theologians and ecclesiastics who belong themselves to the old story. The skills of narration, of storytelling, belong where they have always belonged, in the hands and minds and visions of the imaginers and form-givers, the poets and artists, painters and sculptors, novelists and playwrights, composers, choreographers and cinematographers, philosophers and thinkers whose task it has always been to give shape and form and meaning to the bits and pieces of life in a changing world, to show us the forests that we have trouble seeing for the confusing variety of the trees, to show us the larger landscape that we share with the inhabitants of other forests.

I believe that the new story is already being written, even if it is still waiting in the wings, even if it has not yet coalesced into the shareable whole that will allow it to take center stage in our imaginations as the new community story of who we are, our new "shared cosmology." And I believe that even though it will probably be a long time before the new story has been written on our minds with the clarity to become the defining narrative by which we explain ourselves to ourselves, it is possible already to see something of what it will be like.

The new story will be a universal story rather than a tribal story. It will not be a Christian story nor a Jewish story nor an Islamic story nor a Bhuddist story nor a Hindu story.

It will not be a Western story nor an Eastern story. It will be, it must be, a story appropriate to the new realities of life on this shrinking, globalized planet. It must speak to, and in the voice of, the whole human community.

The new story will be told by employing new metaphors that will enable us to lay hold upon, to think about, to share with each other a daily sense of the mystery and the meaning of our existence. It will not be a story of supernatural gods made in our own image who break in upon our days from somewhere else to save us from our earthy, muddy predicaments. Those old metaphors have seen their day, and though, as yet, the new ones have not been born, I believe that they are even now in their gestation period.

The new story will have at its core a morality that is based upon the *fact* of a single tree of life. It will be a story of our connectedness. The old notion of the "brotherhood of man" is not an ideal to which we should aspire; it is a genetic reality. And the rules of ethical behavior in every realm of life, according to this story, will not be derived from an externally imposed divine law; they will grow out of the mutual respect that seems so proper and natural in the single family unit, because there *is* only one family unit, and it includes every living thing on earth. The moral implications of that simple fact would seem to be enormous.

And finally the new story will be one that is in harmony with the knowledge that scientists have opened to us. Despite the cries and alarms from those who desperately cling to the shell of the old story, the war between science and religion that has raged off and on since the days of Copernicus and Galileo is over. The new story will take for granted as starting points the new cosmology of this ancient, expanding universe and the miracle of human evolution.

In an earlier chapter I wrote of my imaginary journey back down the paths of time, past where my personal family genealogy ran out of material, past the story of my Western cultural antecedents, stumbling blindly through medieval and prehistoric darkness, finally to that remote time when my original parents crossed the evolutionary bridge into full humanness. As important as that journey of the mind is for our understanding of who we are now, it is, I believe, only a small part of the new story that is being written. To fully appreciate the significance of this pivotal "moment" in the autobiography of our species, as important as this new beginning was, we need to understand, of course, that it was not the beginning at all. If an understanding of this "hinging moment" points us to the future of all that we would become as a race, it also points us back to all that we have been before *Homo sapiens* evolved. For if there is only one family tree, there is also only one family history. And it goes all the way back, roughly four billion years, to that initial "spark" of life that occurred in the fecund seas of our adolescent earth. And farther even than that. For if there is but one family history, there is also only one process by which everything that has ever existed came to be, and that process goes all the way back through eons of geological and cosmological time to that mysterious first beginning that scientists, for now, refer to as the Big Bang.

The formulators of the old story didn't have access to

all the information now available to us about that process by which life on earth came to be. I think they must have seen only their uniqueness in contrast to other forms of life around them and that was what they focused on in telling their story. In answer to the Who-am-I? Where-did-I-come-from? questions, based on what they could see around them, I think they just could not get past the notion that, since they were so different, they must have been created specially and separately. If that was so, as it seemed at that time to be, then there must have been a creator who also existed separately from his creation. That's what they told stories about and sang about and based their laws upon and passed down to us as religious belief. And that has been a comforting story. But the time has come to tell another one. So...

> ...*tell me a new story, and...*
> ...*don't leave anything out!*

NO MAGIC KINGDOM

Connecting with the Mystery

I DID NOT LEARN TO PRAY IN CHURCH. Despite my thorough absorption in the life of my church as a young person, the most I learned about praying was the words of the Lord's Prayer, to bow my head and close my eyes while the preacher intoned aloud his supplications to the Heavenly Father, and that I was supposed to thank God for all the good things He had given me and to ask Him to help those who were less fortunate than I. I learned a lot of formulas and words for communicating with the divine being, but I never had any deeply felt sense that all of those words connected me to anything beyond the sound of my own religiosity. Nor did I learn to pray "at my mother's knee," as it were. The only thing I learned about prayer in my parents' home was that fathers, as heads of the household, were supposed to mumble a formulaic blessing at the beginning of every family meal. Other than that, my parents seemed to believe that their religious duty to their two sons was to enforce the rules of Christian behavior. They took us to church "religiously," but the praying part was left to the preacher. Of course, the popular religious culture the Bible Belt where I grew up had a lot to say about prayer, but it was mostly in the form of slogans that were bandied about, like, "The family that prays together stays together," or "Prayer changes things." I remember a popular song urging one to "Talk to the Man Upstairs" and, during World War II, a song about combat pilots "Coming Home on a Wing and a Prayer." And whenever there was a natural disaster, a tornado or hurricane or flood, the television and radio news reporters always found people to interview who believed their lives had been spared because they had prayed to God in the midst of peril.

When I began this book, I knew that at some point I would have to address the business of praying. How could one write about human spirituality and religious faith without discussing prayer? At the very heart of all religious practice lies some form of intercourse, communion, interaction between the believer and the object of his or her belief. Faced, however, with the task of writing something honest and meaningful about that core experience, I found that, in spite of my religious background and my education and experience as a teaching elder in the church, I had no clue as to where to start. Was it that I had simply gotten out of the practice of prayer in the intervening years since I had left the religious profession? No, the truth is, I have to confess, I really had never been "in the practice of prayer." I was somewhat relieved when my brother, after retiring from a long career, also as a Presbyterian minister, confessed to me that he, too, had always found the notion of prayer to be a baffling and troubling matter. That should not have been a surprise, considering that we came from parents whose practice of religion was more a matter of institutional conformity than of personal spirituality and that, for both of us, the decision to go into the ministry came as much from our responses to subtle but persistent family expectations as from any deeply felt personal sense of divine calling. But the fact that I had company in my ignorance did not provide me with much help in thinking about the subject.

Just about the time I was beginning seriously to wrestle with this dilemma, Lenda and I were invited to a buffet luncheon at which one of the guests was the hostess' pastor. Before we filled our plates he was asked to "say the blessing." He began with the obligatory expressions of gratitude for the happy occasion, and went on to thank God for all of the blessings that He had bestowed upon those present (which, since this was a rather typical American upper-middle-class group of folks, were too numerous to catalog), as well as, of course, "...for the bountiful meal, of which we are about to partake." Then, almost as a second thought, he added an appeal to the Heavenly Father to keep us mindful of the starving and ravaged people of the Darfur region of Africa. Upon that note, we all sat down to enjoy our lunch. I don't know that anyone else was paying enough attention to take note of the abrupt change in tone that the prayer had taken (I confess that my on-and-off history with regard to institutional religion tends to make me sensitive to the way things are said and done in a traditional religious context). But I felt that the pastor's introduction of the Darfur tragedy into an ordinary blessing before a meal lent to it a strangely jarring and discordant note. Not because he had sneaked in a little sermonizing under the guise of addressing the deity.

The clergy are often guilty of that little bit of deception: preaching to the congregation when they're supposed to be talking to God. Nor did I think there was anything insincere or hypocritical about his attempt to get these wealthy and comfortable people to feel some concern for a desperately massive case of human suffering. I believe that he truly was troubled by the great gulf that exists between the blessedness of our situation and the cursedness of the lives of the people of Darfur.

On the contrary, the jarring dissonance that disturbed that lovely morning for me had more to do with the theology that lay behind the pastor's words. There was certainly nothing extraordinary or nontraditional in the words he used to address the divine being. Indeed, they were the kinds of pious words that seem to pour off the tongues of practiced clergymen with total facility. And he was talking to the God that most of us in this culture were brought up to believe in. There is this divine personage, we have been taught, who lives up there somewhere, invisible yet available to us. He made us and everything that exists, and He constantly tends to his creation, taking a personal interest in the welfare of every individual child of His. We can talk to Him (pray) and He will hear us, and if we trust in Him, He will come to our aid in time of trouble. That brings to mind another Bible verse I memorized in Sunday school: "Every good and perfect gift is from above, and cometh down from the Father" (James 1: 17 KJV). As believers, we have been taught to acknowledge that He is the source of all the good things that we have been given, which, we must assume, includes all our material wealth, money, cars, homes, clothing, food, medicines, every *thing*, as well as those intangibles like love and friendship and family ties. And we give thanks to him for all of that. And that seems to many of us a very nice thing to believe. That is, until someone has the temerity to include in a prayer of thanksgiving a subject like Darfur. That raises an uncomfortable question. Is this Father-God, who is the source of "every good and perfect gift" that comes our way, this divine personage who intervenes in our lives because He cares for all of His children as individuals, not also the God of the Sudanese? (I understand that many of the people of Darfur are Christians.) If so, He doesn't seem to care for His creation with much evenhandedness. And if it is He who gives to *me* all the good things that *I* enjoy, then He is also the source of all those "good and perfect gifts" that *they* enjoy, the catalog of which would seem to be pitifully short. So, why am I so much more greatly blessed than they, and what is wrong with this picture? Does there not seem to be a problem here with our comfortable belief in this divine benefactor-person?

I believe it is the same problem that was exposed so dramatically by PBS's remarkable documentary film *Faith and Doubt at Ground Zero*.[1] In this captivating and revelatory piece of television journalism, the writers, producers, filmmakers, and director managed to avoid almost completely the temptation to impose their own spin on a painfully sensitive subject, allowing a score of interviewees simply to talk freely before the camera about how September 11 impacted their religious feelings and beliefs. There were survivors, relatives of victims, firemen and policemen, witnesses, writers, and photographers who recorded the event, and a number of professional religious leaders and theologians, ministers, priests, rabbis, even an Islamic cleric. The responses to the question posed by the film, "Where was God on September 11?" ranged from professions of belief that God had been with them on that day to despairing resignation and anger that He had abandoned them:

A woman whose daughter was killed in the first attack said she saw a bright light shining in her window that night and that she concluded it was an angel come to tell her that her daughter was in heaven: "...I never questioned why God didn't intervene...I've asked why he took her...but I felt that God knew best."

Two men who made it out alive, after one rescued the other, described their survival and their new friendship as gifts from God. The first man: "...so, here I am running, screaming like everyone else...my Lord upheld this building and we were in perfect safety, and then the building collapsed...and here I am *God-delivered* (italics mine), and I'm angry...because all those good people were left in this building. They perished, so I'm angry." The second man: "Just like He intervenes in everybody's life, God intervened in my life that day...I couldn't predict what He was going to do...whatever God's plan is, was, and shall be...*is, was*, and shall *be!*"

The wife of a lost fireman spoke of being in Hawaii three months after the attack where she had gone seeking solace with some of her husband's coworkers and other victims' loved ones, and watching a Pacific sunrise: "...such startling beauty that I couldn't believe that this God that I had talked to in my own way for thirty-five years could make this most beautiful place and then turn that loving man into bones...I couldn't reconcile the difference between those two extremes, and I guess that's when I felt that my faith was so weakened by 9/11...God was just not present in me the way He had been before...all I feel at this point is a profound absence of God. I can't bring myself to speak to Him anymore because I feel so abandoned."

A security guard who barely escaped the falling building found himself baffled and angry: "I really can't see the purpose why all these people had to die. I can't accept this. Right now God's not giving me that comfort...I let loose at God. I fired all my barrels at Him. It might sound crazy, but I cursed Him. I damned Him. I think God could have just ended this all. That's why I feel strongly that I'm losing respect for Him...I look at Him now as a barbarian...I think I'm a good Christian, but I have a different view of Him now..."

A young Episcopal priest voiced his desolation: "After September 11 the face of God was a blank slate for me. God couldn't be counted on the way that I trusted in Him before... That's what I felt as I stood at ground zero. God seemed absent...That was frightening because all the attributes that I had counted on had been stripped away..."

Of all the responses on the part of professional religious leaders, one of the most moving was that of Orthodox Rabbi Brad Hirschfield. It deserves to be quoted in full: "Since September 11 people keep asking me, 'Where was God?' They think that because I'm a rabbi I have answers. And I actually think that my job as a rabbi is to help them live with those questions. If God's ways are mysterious, then live with the mystery. It's upsetting, it's scary, it's painful, it's deep, but it's interesting. No plan! That's what mystery is. It's all of those things. You want plan? Then tell me about plan. But if you're going to tell me about how the plan saved you, you better also be able to explain how the plan killed them. And the test of that has nothing to do with saying it in your synagogue or church. The test of that has to do with going and saying it to someone who has just buried someone and telling them that it was God's plan to blow their loved one apart. Look at them and say to them that it was God's plan for their children to go to bed every night for the rest of their lives without a parent. And if you can say that…well, at least you're honest. *I don't worship the same God* (italics mine), but that, at least, has integrity. It's just that it's too easy. That's my problem with the answer; not that I think they're being inauthentic when they say it, or that they're dishonest. It's just too damned easy! It's easy because it gets God off the hook, and it's easy because it gets their religious belief off the hook. And right now everything is on the hook!"

If you are going to tell me how God's plan saved you, then you are going to have to explain how and why His plan included the deaths of all those others. If you're going to persist in believing that this personal God intervened in the midst of this disaster to single you out and rescue you, then you are obliged to explain to the loved ones of those three thousand who died (who were probably praying as desperately as you were) why He did not intervene to rescue

them. If you are going to continue to believe in this divine
father-benefactor who is the source of "every good and
perfect gift" that you personally, as an upper-middle-class
American, enjoy, then you need to explain to the people of
Darfur why He doesn't care for them. And if you are so sure
that your prayers to God, as that tornado bore down on
your neighborhood, caused Him to spare your home and
family, then you are surely obligated to go down the street
the next day to ask your neighbors to forgive you for causing
God to change the path of the storm so that it destroyed *their*
home and killed *their* loved ones.

The problem here is precisely the one that the rabbi hit
upon when he protested, "I don't worship the same God."
There are different ways of thinking and speaking about
the ultimate mystery of the universe and our life in it, and
those who glibly spoke in response to 9/11 about "God's
plan" and God intervening on their behalf have a different
concept of that mystery than the one with which the rabbi is
comfortable. For those respondents in the documentary who
expressed a feeling of abandonment, loss of faith, anger
at God, or bewilderment at his absence, what was really
tested by the events of September 11 and found wanting
was not God, but their image of God—their metaphor for
God—as this personal "problem-solver in the sky" who
was not supposed to let this kind of terrible thing happen
("...I believe God could have ended all of this..."). And for
those who were able to cling to their belief in a God who
had stepped in to save them personally from the death and
destruction all around them ("My Lord upheld this building

and we were in perfect safety…"), well, I think the rabbi is right: their convenient image of a God who selectively intervenes like that is "just too damned easy." It lets them off the hook of having to confront the unanswerable questions and uncomfortable contradictions raised by such tragic events as the attack on the twin towers, or the capriciousness of a tornado's path, or the kind of genocide that was taking place in Darfur.

How one prays and what one expects in the way of answers to prayer—when the buildings of an ordered life are falling down all around, when the storms of life are threatening, or the inequities of life are rattling the comfortable foundations—are totally dependent upon the *kind* of God one worships, or—to put it another way— upon the particular metaphor or metaphors that one employs when thinking about or talking about what is ultimately true about the universe and our life in it. That is generally what we mean when we use the word "God." It is the generic term, the primary metaphor, the main figure of speech, we use when we are talking about what we believe to be ultimately true about the universe and our life in it. The function of the word with the capital "G" is to focus us on the ultimate mystery and meaning of existence. The main problems with that word, as we use it today, are the *secondary* metaphors that have attached themselves to it, that have congealed around it to freeze it in one form, one image, and rob it of growth. And that, simply put, is the problem with much of what passes as religious faith today: we are living in the twenty-first century with a medieval notion of God.

I don't believe that prayer is about getting things we want or think we need from our Big Daddy upstairs because I don't believe there is a Big Daddy upstairs. We do not live in a magic kingdom where all we have to do is click our heels together or assume the proper posture or say the right words for everything to be all right. There is no great "problem solver in the sky" ready to come to our rescue when things get out of hand. It may make some of us feel better to call upon a higher power when we are trembling with fear in the path of an oncoming storm, but the facts are that tornadoes and hurricanes behave according to their own thermodynamic laws, and I don't believe those laws include a sensitivity to who is praying in what house or to which God. The death and destruction of 9/11 had more to do with a few individuals' angry reaction to the past failings of the West in general, and of the United States in particular, to deal equitably with the people of the Middle East than it did with the failure of our tribal deity—in whom we have trusted to "Bless the USA"—to come to our rescue. And isn't it a strange concept of God, anyway, that defines Him as a separate creator-being out there who made the whole vast universe, but who is yet willing to fiddle around with the laws of nature or the dynamics of human history just because some of His children are flinging some fearful words in his direction?

I believe that prayer and, for that matter, the whole of religious activity—however we are accustomed to defining it, or practicing it (or rejecting its cheaper forms)—is, at heart, an expression of the deep hunger that gnaws at the spirit of every human for a sense of connection to the mysterious *Life* that animates the universe and of which we are a unique, if somewhat troubled and contradictory, expression. I believe that one of the things that happened to our species when we hesitatingly shuffled across the evolutionary bridge from *Homo erectus* to *Homo sapiens* was that we lost our natural, undifferentiated sense of belonging to the zoological world that had given us life and to the botanical world that had nourished us and ultimately to the mysterious vitality of the universe, out of whose elemental furnace all that exists was forged. We *did* become like gods in our capacity to know ourselves and to stand outside the natural house where we were born and look upon it as an object of curiosity and a subject of investigation. But it is lonely out here, and we have never ceased to coddle the dream—a vision now timeworn and somewhat vague—of a beautiful and luxurious garden that we think we remember as our nursery in the innocence of our species' infancy. But we can never go back; we can never re-cross that bridge. However much that primordial simplicity may seem to call to us, we have a fuller, more challenging life to live than is possible in a heavenly paradise (or in a natural Eden) and work to do building a new kind of garden on earth. But even as we go about that human task, our personal hunger for a sense of belonging to a larger reality, one that transcends our small selves and our few days on the planet, will not let us be (one way to explain the universality of religious feeling?). We seem to be dogged by a deep racial memory of wholeness and harmony with the universe. And we ache for the old home place. And can that hunger ever begin to be assuaged, or is such hope merely

No Magic Kingdom

the dream of starry-eyed romantics? Is that completeness
and connection, which sounds so appealing, only an escapist
illusion, a fantasy for those who cannot face the hard truth
of a cold and meaningless universe? For many, that may
seem to be the tough reality. And is the notion that we might
actually know and participate in a *Life* that transcends our
own simply the hallucinatory product of a religious opiate?
Based upon some of the religion we see practiced around us
today, one could not be blamed for arriving at that despairing
conclusion. But I dare to think that such despair is not the
only possibility. I dare to believe that the hunger is real and
legitimate and, what is more, that it can be nourished. There
is such a thing as an answer to prayer, but not the one we
have imagined.

We usually think of prayer as something *we* do, as if
prayer were up to us, as if we were the initiating parties
in a bargaining transaction between us and some remote
power. It's up to us to start the intercourse or we won't get
what we pray for—like saying the magic words. But what
if it were the other way around? What if the "current " of
prayer—the connecting tide—flowed not *from* us but *to* us?
What if the whole universe were reaching out to us, inviting
us into connection with itself? I believe that something like
that could well be true. The poet Mark Jarman speaks of
that invitation in one of his *Unholy Sonnets*:

> Look into the darkness and the darkness looks—
> As if it massed before a telescope
> Or turned because it heard your step—

The darkness looks at you. This idea spooks
Some people, and their reason self-destructs.
Seized by a love of daylight, back they jump
Into the known, blazing like a headlamp,
Into the senses tuned like cars and trucks.

And what about the counsel of my friend
Who says that when we look for God, remember
God looks for us? If that's what starts the thing,
Then we must drive in circles till we find
It's all one. To be looked for is to look for.
And seeing is believing and being seen.[2]

Could it be that the *Life* that is the life of the world is hungering for us even as we are hungering for it (whether or not we know just what is gnawing at our gut)? Could it be that the *Life* that has spoken us into existence needs our self-consciousness as a continuation of its own being? Could it be that that *Life* (by whatever metaphor you find to describe it or her or him) needs us for its completeness even as we need it for the completion of our own selves—as the lover depends upon his or her beloved for wholeness? Could it be that our longings for wholeness, connection, and communion are simply vibrations along the sinews of our spirits in response to the chorus of that universal *Life* that is calling us into empathy with itself? And could this be the real meaning of prayer, that prayer and the answer to prayer, calling out and being called, seeing and being seen, are one and the same experience? And which part comes first?

No Magic Kingdom

In one of Annie Dillard's collections of writings, *Teaching a Stone to Talk*, the title essay explores the eccentric behavior of one of her acquaintances, "Larry...a man in his thirties who lives alone with a stone he is trying to teach to talk." It is a "palm-sized oval beach cobble," which he takes down from its shelf every day in order to engage with it in some undescribed ritual aimed at teaching it to speak. She writes that she doesn't think that "he expects the stone to speak as we do, and describe for us its long life...I think instead that he is trying to teach it to say a single word, such as 'cup,' or 'uncle.'"[3] Now, some of Ms. Dillard's readers might conclude that her friend Larry has swung a few degrees too far away from plumb, that perhaps he's been living too long alone in the woods. My diagnosis, however, is that Larry is merely suffering from a seriously limited imagination and sadly constricted expectations. He is, of course, wasting his time trying to teach a stone to speak, presumably in English. What he needs to be doing is teaching himself to listen to what the stone, by its very existence in that cobbled form, is already trying to say to him.

The world is populated from top to bottom, in and out, everywhere we turn our eyes and ears, by a chorus of voices innumerable and infinitely varied, each busily singing its part in a boisterous oratorio in celebration of *Life*. But we don't seem to be listening. We seem almost tone deaf to the song of invitation the world is singing to us. We seem almost blind to the "sounds of silence," the voices of color and form, the blending harmony of the green-robed ensemble, the vibrant dance of stalk and limb and leaf that move to the accompaniment of the wind. We just don't seem to believe any longer that all of that flowering and flying, growing and multiplying, budding and dying and being born again, which the "natural" world is always engaging in, has anything to do with us. We treat all of that like mere background noise that we tune out in order to hear the lonely little songs we sing to ourselves. Our senses, according to the poet, being "tuned like cars and trucks," are so blinded by the headlights of the familiar that any beacon that reaches out to us from beyond our immediate well-lit circle is lost in the light pollution of our electric artificiality. But while there may indeed be some who are genuinely deaf to any sounds but the clattering and clumping of their own trudging transit from birth to death, or any songs but the boring echoes of their own voices, most of us are more like Larry and his pet rock: our imaginations are dulled by preconceived notions and our expectations are badly constricted.

I have already written generally about my early passion for birds. Go back with me now to a specific day, a clear, crisp Saturday morning in the fall of 1948, to a place called Edgewood Lake on the southern perimeter of the city of Birmingham, Alabama. At one time, it had been a moderately large body of water created by the damming of a stream that ran through the second valley south of where the city had grown up between two containing ridges of hills and mountains. For some reason, the decision had been made some years earlier to drain the lake, and so it was just a low-lying, mostly dry bed, thickly overgrown with willows and marshy grass. Along the roads that marked its borders there was the uneven cadence of a tree line of pines, maples, sweet gums, and water oaks, and through it, the remains of the original stream wandered randomly as if in search of a path through this newly grown up wilderness, occasionally pausing to widen out into a small pond before moving on in its painstakingly casual exploration. And it was populated by a thrilling variety of birds. Great blue and green herons were almost always to be seen, along with rusty and red-winged blackbirds, harriers and red-shouldered hawks, yellow-throats and swamp sparrows, pied-billed grebes and coots, several species of ducks in the fall and winter, and the occasional spotted sandpiper or other inland shore birds. On this particular morning, as was my usual Saturday practice, I had gotten up before dawn, slurped down a quick breakfast, hung my binoculars around my neck, crammed my *Peterson's Field Guide* into the side pocket of my war-surplus army field jacket, and was on my bicycle heading for the lake as the sun was coming up. It was only a pedal of two or so miles from my house to the place where I stashed my bike, concealed amongst a stand of willows, so that by six o'clock I was ready to begin my quest.

Bird-watching (or birding—the currently preferred word for the practice) had been for me, from the very beginning, a mostly solitary pursuit. Occasionally I enjoyed a group outing with other members of the Birmingham Audubon Club, but I was never happier in those teen years than when I was alone in the woods or fields with only my binoculars and field guide. Birding has often been compared to hunting without a gun, but that's not really an apt comparison at all. Except for those unusual occasions when one goes to a specific place to see some particular species that reportedly has been spotted there, the average birder most often doesn't know precisely what he is looking for. And that is the whole point and the joy of it. What he is looking for and expecting is always a surprise. So, I had learned to walk softly and to move deliberately, head turning from side to side, finger ready on the focus wheel of my binoculars, continually on the alert for eccentric movements in trees, bushes and grass, or the sudden flash of color that announces a bird's presence. I had learned the discipline of silence, necessary if one is to pick up on the scratching and rustling sounds of birds in the brush, or the varied vocabulary of rattles, buzzes, chirps, peeps, chucks, calls, and lyrical vocalizations that make up bird communication. I had learned to stand or sit or crouch unmoving for long periods, knowing that there was nothing I could do to force the issue, that I could only wait patiently for the bird that I hoped and believed was in that tree or behind that bush or in that tall grass to decide to show itself. And that kind of patient expectation hardly ever went unrewarded.

On the particular morning I am remembering, I had already been out for an hour or more. The sun was well above the horizon by now, though the air still retained the brittle clarity and coolness that seems to be the universal hallmark of autumn. I had been following the wandering course of the stream, staying as far up on the bank as possible to avoid the soggy mud closer to the water's edge. Whatever birds I had already identified had no doubt been delightful and beautiful, but not so remarkable as to be specifically recalled from this distance in time. I had come upon one of the many small ponds that dotted the dry lake bed and was searching the opposite bank for anything that might be feeding at the water's edge or lurking in the tall grass when I caught a movement out of the periphery of my left eye. Turning, I saw, just a few feet above the willows and marsh reeds at the far end of the pond, a small flight of ducks coming right at me with that intensely muscular and rapidly purposeful style of flying that all ducks seem to exhibit, as if they are always in a hurry to get where they are going. Hoping that they might be coming in to land on the pond, and fearing that my obvious presence would startle them off, I dropped quickly to a prone position. I can still see my khaki-clad arms, bent at the elbows to protect my binoculars, sinking into the dark mud up to the cuffs and armpits of my army field jacket. But I made no move to extract myself from the gooey muck. I was welded to the spot, not just by the mud, but by the spectacle of six male blue-winged teals making a web-feet-down landing less than five yards from where I lay. Their pale blue epaulettes rivaled the intensity of the morning sky as they flashed by so closely, but then they were suddenly concealed from view as they settled onto the surface of the water and folded their wings neatly into their speckled brown "side pockets." The brilliant white crescent-shaped patches that fill the space between the eye and the beak of the blue-wing drake seemed more like wild exclamation points against their dark slate blue facial feathers than the ordinary commas that they more closely resembled.

The blue-winged teal is not a rare bird. Over the years I have seen hundreds of them. But on that day those six small ducks might have been the last remnants of a disappearing species, so great was my thrill at their sudden appearance, and so total was the transformation that I experienced because of their gift of intimate proximity. In that moment I was delivered—most obviously from the immediate discomfort of the wet and smelly mud into which I had thrown myself—but also lifted up from the tangle of my sixteen-year-old adolescence, from the stress of teen-parent wrestling, from the troubling ache of always being five years behind my peers in physical development, and from gnawing apprehension about ever finding a place in the world where I could fit. All of that, at least for the moment, was gone. I was instantly alive and free and more peacefully me than I had ever been. I was okay. I was whole. I was complete. And I was exhilarated by my very existence. The totally unpredictable advent of those astonishingly beautiful birds, the wonder of my nearness to creatures so free, so completely alive, and so in harmony with their environment, was like a sacrament, an epiphany. I was touched by something larger than me and my petty anxieties. It was as if the universe itself had welcomed me, had reached out to me in a brief and inviting gesture of recognition. I didn't fully understand at the time what had happened to me, nor the significance of what I was experiencing. I didn't understand then that my overwhelming sense of release, of wholeness and connection, was something like prayer and the answer to prayer in its deepest and most profound sense. The next day being Sunday, I was back in church again with my family doing our weekly religious duty. I am quite sure that the afterglow of that encounter at the lake was still with me (as it is even now, sixty years later), but I never saw then that it had anything to do with what went on in church. My life in the natural world—the passion with which I pursued my interest in birds—and my religious life, which I pursued dutifully if not passionately, seemed to be separately compartmentalized with little possibility of overlap. And that is the way it remained for most of my life.

Now, please understand, I do not believe that there was anything magical or mystical or providential about the advent of those six little ducks on that autumn morning so long ago. There was nothing intentional or purposeful in their decision to land on the particular pond, next to which I just happened to be standing. And had I not had the presence of mind to make myself less obvious by dropping down prone in that waterside muck, they would probably have been startled away and would have landed on some other pond and my encounter with them would never have taken place. That was a totally random happening. *The only thing that made it special was my expectation.* Remember, as I said earlier, I was in that place for the sole purpose of being surprised. I didn't know what I was looking for specifically on that particular Saturday morning, but I was fully expecting something wonderful to appear. I couldn't make any bird show itself to me—common or rare, plain or spectacular. I could only practice the discipline that I had learned from long hours in the field: be quiet, be alert to everything that moves, and wait patiently and actively for something to happen. And when it did happen, when those elegant little ducks landed so close to me that morning, I was literally beside myself with the thrill of their sudden appearance. The wonder and the joy of that moment was all-consuming, and in giving myself over to it, I experienced a wholeness and a completeness that descriptive words have not the power to dissect or explain. Suffice it to say, I was connected. The life that was me and the life of those wonderfully beautiful birds and, through them, out to the larger natural world and to the whole expansive life of the universe, all the way to the Big Bang and back again, back through autumn sunlight and blue-winged teals and me, even to the microscopic creatures that made a living soup of the mud in which I was partially immersed—were all one reality!

When I began writing this chapter, I turned to the dictionary (always a good starting point on almost any subject) for a definition of "prayer," and I was surprised to discover that the word "prayer" comes from the same Latin root as the word "precarious," which means, "uncertain, unstable, insecure, dependent on circumstances beyond our control; dependent on the will or pleasure of another; liable to be withdrawn or lost at the will of another." Now, "precarious" is not a word that usually comes to mind when one thinks about the benefits of religious faith. The life of the believer is not supposed to be precarious; religious faith is supposed to comfort and reassure and bring a sense of peace and security. Yet, when I listened to the religious testimonies of those witnesses, survivors, and family members of the victims of the 9/11 disaster, the word "precarious" seemed peculiarly appropriate to describe how they felt about their lives in the aftermath of that awful day. For most of them, their faith had not afforded them its promised comfort and reassurance. And even for those whose faith remained strong—most of whom had been "miraculously" spared— there were profound contradictions in their reports on the deity's performance in response to their desperate entreaties. He was there for some but not for others. He saved some but not others. He held the building up until a few had escaped, but then He let it fall. He could have ended it, but He didn't. His "plan" apparently allowed people to live and to die rather indiscriminately. That same sense of precariousness seems to apply when faithful people are caught up in natural calamities like tornadoes, floods, and hurricanes, or in human disasters like Darfur. If the "Man Upstairs" is really in charge, and if He really listens to the cries of his human children, His responses seem terribly fickle. Maybe those victims were not praying hard enough, or were using the wrong words. Maybe they weren't sincere enough or righteous enough or Christian enough. But all of that seems so fundamentally petty, and pettiness is the last attribute we would look for in a description of deity. No, I think the rabbi got it right; it all depends upon the kind of God your faith imagines. And the metaphor of God as a kind of heavenly problem solver, the understanding of religion as a kind of escape clause in ones contract with life, and the definition of prayer as a magical formula for getting what you think you need, all belong to that old story, whose basic inadequacies seem increasingly apparent.

My dictionary, however, also contains a second definition of the word prayer that departs completely from that sense of precarious dependence upon an arbitrary external power: to pray, according to this second definition, is "to enter into spiritual communion with God or an object of worship." There is a problem with that definition also, of course, in its presumptive use of the words "God" and "object of worship," but if we can get past those timeworn figures of speech, what remains is a notion of prayer as a state of being, a way of living in vital connection with that mysterious *Life* of which we and all else that exists are expressions. Is it really possible to "enter into communion with" such a reality as a *Life* that transcends our own time and flesh-bound existence? I believe that it is, if we are willing to look and listen for *Life's* approach to us.

Expectation, of course, is the key, for, the truth is, we will not hear what we're not expecting to hear and we won't see what we cannot imagine will appear to us. The sounds and sights of the world around us will form themselves into an intelligible language of connection only if we are expecting them to speak to us. If we remain deaf to the possibility of their speech, then they will stay locked away from us in their dumbness. I admit that it is easy to tune out the varied expressions of *Life's* presence with us; there is just so much of it, so much color, so many sounds, so much frenetic activity, so much stuff demanding our attention. Somehow we have developed the habit of thinking of the world of nature as a sort of parallel universe to our own, one that only touches us tangentially on occasions. No wonder we find it easier just to turn a deaf ear and a blind eye to the sights and sounds of the natural world; our human world is crowded enough as it is. But it is just that dichotomy between the so-called natural world and our separate human world that I believe we must find ways to overcome. Our own spiritual health and the health of our home place are demanding that we take steps to heal that rift. The evolutionary scientists have shown us the truth about ourselves, that we are part of nature, that we are products of the same processes that resulted in all other forms of life, from earthworms to elephants, from green algae to great apes. And to the degree that we are separated and alienated from the natural world and its citizens, we will be alienated also from our true selves, and we will find ourselves as strangers in the habitat that is our only true home, the living world in which we have our true being.

To let oneself go in wonder and celebration of the beauty and the mystery of *Life's* presence around us is to experience a sense of wholeness and connectedness with the universe that can change one's life. I know that to be true. The spiritual function of wonder is to break us loose from our reticence, to free us from the dragging anchors of cynicism and unbelief, to yank us out of inhibited self-regard into the ecstatic freedom of total responsiveness. Letting go of oneself in a moment of awe-inspired release can be a saving grace. And this is the point at which prayer and the answer to prayer really merge into one experience. This letting go, this release from anxious reticence, is the means by which we may reforge our connection with that *Life* that is the life of the whole universe. I believe that we are being called into empathy and a sense of kinship with all those inhabitants of our universal home, animate and inanimate, who share with us the same pulsing energy that gives being to us all. We are not alone. We are part of an enormous extended family. And we're being invited to a great celebratory reunion. That sense of connection is what I experienced on the muddy bank of that pond on that autumn day long ago when my blue-winged teals came for me, and no matter how many times in my life I have lost my way in the darkness of anxious fear and self-pitying isolation, somehow I have always known that I could return to that same spiritual moment of expectation and surprise at some other wild meeting place and the connection would be restored.

I believe that there is truth to the poet's assertion that when we look into the darkness, as thick and opaque as the darkness often seems, there is *Life* there that looks back at us. I believe, further, that the "current" of what we have called prayer—the tide of connection with that transcendent *Life*—mainly flows not *from* us but *to* us. I believe that the medium of *Life's* approach to us is life itself, the life we share with each other and all our kin on the evolutionary tree, as well as the life of the botanical world that sustains us, and the physical, geological life of the cosmos. *Life* calls to life. We have only to open ourselves to its invitation.

THE LAST CHAPTER

Where do we go from here?

This is going to be brief because, at this point, I really do not know what I am talking about. I have absolutely no experience to draw upon for what I am about to discuss. This is the last chapter, and the last chapter is about, well, the last chapter. And, of course, my own last chapter has not yet been lived, but when I have lived it and it is over, I'm not going to get back here to tell anyone about it, so all I can do is guess at what the last chapter will be like. Here's what I suspect.

In the not too distant future I am going to take my leave of this earthly existence; I am gong to die. Or, as Hamlet put it so colorfully, I'm going to "shuffle off this mortal coil" (I love that; it sounds like something that happens on a vaudeville stage, like "shuffling off to Buffalo.") That much I do know. I hope, of course, like everybody else, that my exit will not be too painful or, what's probably worse, too embarrassing, but I don't know how much control I will have over that. Not much, I suspect. In that matter, I can only hope for the best. But there is no doubt whatsoever about the end. It is coming, and relatively soon for me. And what happens after that? Well, I pretty much know what will happen to my body. My wife and

I decided some time ago that we would donate our bodies to the Vanderbilt University Medical School for use by students of anatomy. Because both her parents did the same thing, we know that when the young future doctors have learned all they can by dissecting what's left of us, the remains will be cremated and the ashes will be returned to the family (if they want them) in cardboard cartons that look like plain versions of a Kentucky Fried Chicken family-sized bucket. If no one has any particular need to have my ashes around the house, the medical school will see that they are buried in a discreet cemetery plot, which the university owns for that purpose (they even hold a very dignified and appreciative group memorial service for the families and friends of those whose ashes they are returning). Thus will I return to the earth, "ashes to ashes and dust to dust." The notion that my worn out body should be chemically pickled and buried in an expensive metal coffin enclosed in a waterproof vault seems almost obscene to me, a ridiculous waste of money and effort that would accomplish nothing but to slow down the inevitable decay and prevent the natural recycling of what's left of me. After all is said and done and over with, don't the worms deserve their fair share of my used up flesh? At the very least, my ashes might have some little bit of nutritional value, if only as fertilizer.

Christians, of course, have always believed that there is life after the death of the body. There seems to be some confusion, however, as to precisely what kind of life is implied by that notion. Are we, for instance, to look forward to some kind of spiritual life that commences immediately at the moment of the body's expiration? That would seem to be what is implied by the common euphemism for death as "passing," or by the oft-heard assurance at the death of a loved one that "we know he is in a better place." This seems to suggest a belief that if the person who dies has been a "good Christian," he or she will go immediately to heaven where, as an elderly friend who is close to the end of life was quoted in response to a question about her fear of dying, "I'm not afraid to die because I know my Heavenly Father has prepared a place for me…" So, if, when we die, our souls leave the body and go directly to heaven to be with God, why do Christians cling to a belief, as stated in the Apostles' Creed, in the "resurrection of the body"? At what point are the soul and body reunited, and is the body that is resurrected the one that we just had embalmed and sealed up in a metal vault in the ground? (I suspect that the whole idea of preserving the body after death originated with the notion that somehow we were going to need it in the afterlife. Isn't that why the Egyptians developed the science of mummification?) Some Christians believe that the resurrection will only occur in conjunction the second coming of Christ when the "trumpet will sound" and the "saints" (the saved) will rise from their graves. I would presume that this includes all of the saints, even those buried long ago whose bodies have long since decayed away to dirt and dust and reusable carbon, and not just those who were fortunate enough to have their bodies preserved to some degree by embalming. This does seem to raise a question about why, if the condition of the body is not an issue, Christians should bother with all those enormous funeral expenses. Still, no matter how much confusion may persist regarding the details about just what happens after death, a belief in an afterlife, including rewards for a righteous life here and now and punishment for a sinful one, heaven and hell, have always been central to Western religious faith.

Now, I have to admit that the everlasting life promised in the Christian creed as a prospective reward for my having lived a good life on earth, holds very little appeal for me. On the surface, it sounds more like an eternal life *sentence* than something to which I should look forward with joyous expectation. The notion that I, as a self-conscious individual, must continue to live on forever in some form, somewhere, after my earthly body has finally lost its capacity to sustain life just raises too many dumb questions to make any sense to me. Where will I be? If heaven is a real place somewhere in the universe, how long will it take me to get there, even traveling at the speed of light? If it is not a real place—if it has no "whereness" or "thereness" about it— then what are we talking about? And what will I be doing there? (I never have been any good with stringed instruments!) Will I be the person I am now? Will I know who I am and what's going on around me? Will I recognize other individuals and relate to them in some way? Won't it be terribly crowded? One could object, of course, that such questions are indeed dumb because they rise out of my limited human capacity to imagine the incomparable wonders of heavenly life, and that any attempt to describe the glories of the hereafter are, therefore, useless. Well, maybe so, and, after all, since no one has ever returned to tell us about it, such attempts to imagine or visualize what an afterlife would be like are mere speculation anyway.

Apart from those admittedly dumb questions, however, there are some more serious ones that come to mind. For instance, why *do* we cling so resolutely to our belief in life after death? Why is it so difficult to face the possibility that, for us, as individually self-conscious persons, this life on earth is all there is, and when this is over there is nothing else? Is it precisely because we fear the nothingness and oblivion that death represents? Or is it that we have trouble facing the loss of our individual identities, that such a loss would somehow rob our earthly life of significance and meaning? Many would say, of course, that it is not death they fear but the process of dying, and that makes sense. No one looks forward to the ravages of old age, the likely pain of crippled joints and debilitating disease, and the certain loss of control that dying entails. I've already begun to experience the onset of my physical decline (including a recent double bypass heart operation), and it isn't fun. But believing in an afterlife is not going to change that. Perhaps it is the prospect of being granted "a new lease on youth" in that heavenly place that fosters our faith in the future life. Certainly for many death will come as a deliverance from a life that is difficult to bear, a life of struggle and hardship, disability and pain, poverty and deprivation. That is perhaps the clearest reason of all for clinging to our hope for heaven, the promise that at the end of this time of toil and trouble there will be a better day "in that great gittin' up morning." It was that promise of a better home "on the other side" that made life, if hardly tolerable, at least survivable, for a people dispossessed and robbed of dignity by the crushing cruelties of slavery, as expressed in the celebratory poetry of the great African-American spirituals:

> *I looked over Jordan and what did I see,*
> *Comin' for the carry me home;*
> *A band of angels comin' after me,*
> *Comin' for to carry me home.*

> *Swing low, sweet chariot,*
> *Comin' for to carry me home,*
> *Swing low, sweet chariot,*
> *Comin' for to carry me home.*

To be perfectly honest, though, that sort of degradation has not been part of my experience. To the degree that I am able to empathize with those whose lives have been marked by pain and struggle, deprivation and despair, I can easily understand why they would harbor those deep longings for a better life "over Jordan," but I have been exceedingly fortunate to have lived a life mostly free of pain and struggle. I have found this life to be good and richly satisfying. Oh, there have been the usual irritants, frustrations, and disappointments, but I have known such joy and so much love that when I think of dying, I do not automatically look forward to deliverance into a promised land of heavenly bliss. I am mostly just sorry that my days here in this good place are coming to an end. And that disappointment is all the more poignant because it contains the reality of having to say good-bye to the people I have loved the most, either as they or I reach the end of this road. Perhaps it is that capacity for loving another so deeply, which seems itself to transcend time and circumstance, that feeds the most personal of reasons for hanging on to the hope of being reunited in some better place than this one.

Ultimately, of course, the reason most Christians believe that they will go to heaven when they die is simply that they were taught to believe that. That is, after all, one of the core doctrines upon which Christianity is based, and it is what the New Testament teaches us, isn't it? There are three passages from the Bible that every Christian seems to know by heart, and which together add up to a fairly simple and clear summary of what Christian faith is all about. They have to do with our origins, with how we should live, and with our final destiny. The first, having to do with where we came from, is from the first chapter of Genesis: "In the beginning God created the heavens and the earth..." The second, having to do with the promise of a good life here on earth, is the twenty-third Psalm: "The Lord is my shepherd, I shall not want ..." And the third, which spells out the believer's hope for life after death, is John 3:16: " For God so loved the world that he gave his only Son, that whoever believes in him should not perish but have eternal life." For those who accept the Bible literally as the inspired word of God, that about clinches it with regard to the afterlife. They may wonder about the details—streets of gold, the company of angels, harp playing and all of that—but the big question has been answered. And for the believer, that "blessed assurance" can be mighty comforting. For some of us, though, it isn't quite that easy. For one who believes, as I do, that, however inspired and revered they may be, all books are human in origin and are therefore subject to critical examination and varying interpretations, what the Bible says about life after death is not simply the end of the matter. What, for instance, does this verse from the book of John really mean when it says that whoever believes in him will not perish? What exactly does it mean to believe *in* God's only son? It seems to be saying that if I simply believe that Jesus was, in some sense, the only son of God, then I won't ever die. But that can't be true. Everybody perishes eventually, no matter what they believe, if to perish means simply to die. And if it doesn't mean that, then what does it mean? And what about this word "eternal"? Is that simply to be understood as synonymous with the word "everlasting," which clearly refers to an unending length of time? Or could the word "eternal" be interpreted just as well to be referring to a certain quality of life as opposed to a quantity of time? If so, then perhaps what this is telling us is simply that believing in Jesus will bring to our lives a spiritual quality that lifts us above material and temporal concerns. But then we come back to that troublesome bit about not perishing. So, I don't know. I'm not sure what this most commonly recited Bible verse really means. This was not something that Jesus said of himself. This was written about those who believe in him by some unknown person, many years after his death. So, if the question is even as simple as what Jesus himself taught about life after death, it still doesn't seem to me to be very clear at all. I just don't know.

I don't know. That's about all I can say with any certainty about the last chapter. Where do we go from here? I do not know. Though I can find no compelling reason to believe that I, as a self-conscious individual, will live on in some form or another after my body has finally called it quits, I can't say with any certainty that I won't. But if there is a "great gittin' up morning" for me, it will come as a big surprise. I'm not expecting it. But I just don't *know*. There are some things, however, that I *believe* about this last great unknown, which I have already hinted at in earlier chapters. I *believe* that the world, the universe, is charged through and through with a *Life* energy that is transcendent and unconditional, and I believe that everything that exists is an expression of that *Life*. Everything that lives is an incarnation of that one *Life*. I live in that *Life* and that *Life* lives in me, and in you, and in every animate and inanimate thing that can be said to be alive. In that *Life*, I am one with every other expression of that *Life*. My existence takes its meaning and its significance from the fact that I am an incarnation of that transcendent *Life*. And the *Life* that is in me is unconditional; it is not dependent upon my puny body for its being. The *Life*, of which I am but a minor expression, does not cease to be when my little body wears out, is discarded and returns to the earth from whence it came. The *Life* in which "I live and move and have my being" cannot die unless the universe itself should cease to be. And in the context of my overwhelming sense of belonging to the transcendent *Life*, I also affirm my kinship and my connection with all the other animals and plants and other living forms on our family tree. In affirming my oneness with all my kin in the animal branch of the tree of life, I am also able to embrace my mortality. My death, like that of all the other animals, is part of a natural process and therefore a positive aspect of incarnated life. I do acknowledge, of course, that, as a human being, I occupy a special place in the zoological branch of the evolutionary family. I have been granted a degree of self-awareness that is not available to my animal cousins. But whether or not that unique package of special gifts that *Homo sapiens* enjoy includes a bonus trip to some separate afterlife, in some place of continued self-awareness, I shall just have to wait and see. But I'm not counting on it. In the meantime, as far as the here and now are concerned, I believe that the *Life* that transcends my time-bound existence, the mysterious energy that continues to flow outward to me and through me from the very beginning of being, is always available to me in ways that pass all rational understanding. The poet says that "when we look into the darkness, the darkness looks back at us." I believe that when we look expectantly into the lively world that surrounds us, the *Life* that is the light and life of everything that exists can penetrate my little corner of darkness and draw me into communion with itself. *Life* calls to life. *Life* calls us into communion with itself through life, in life, by means of all the various incarnations of *Life* that surround us everywhere we look. The great mystery of the universe is *Life*. The wonder of my little life is that I am part of that undying mystery that is *Life* itself.

CONCLUSION:
THE GOD WE HAVE IMAGINED

My own "Confession of Faith"

W HEN I WAS PREPARING TO GO OFF to college, an adult friend
gave me a very special book, small in size, modest in length,
written by the British cleric J. B. Phillips. I don't recall now
very much of the book's specific content, but the title alone
still speaks volumes: *Your God is Too Small.*[1] It was just what
I needed to hear at the time, because my Sunday school
religion was about to be challenged by the larger world into
which I was maturing. Briefly put, what that little book taught
me was that my ideas about God *could* and *should* change as
my perceptions of the world changed. And so they have.

As I set out on the quest that became the writing of *this*
little book, I wasn't sure where I would eventually arrive. For
my starting point I had one simple premise, that all religious
language is basically and necessarily metaphorical in nature
(poetic imagery as opposed to literal, factual information),
and the accompanying conviction that we are living,
presently, in an in-between time amidst the dying of the old
metaphors that have for centuries given form and content
to Western religious belief and the birth of new ones more
attuned to modern perceptions of the universe and our
place in it. I believed that we were already experiencing the

increasing emptiness of the old Judeo-Christian story while a new story had not yet appeared. This writing has been a sort of summing up of my spiritual and intellectual journey so far, and as I approach the end of this part of that odyssey, I am more convinced than ever that my initial premise was substantially correct. Nothing in the realm of religious truth can be taken literally because, when we think about or attempt to share with others our sense of the mystery that transcends the everydayness of our lives, we are always attempting to grasp with our minds or to describe in words realities that do not submit to the usual measuring capacities of our ordinary senses. We are trying to describe the indescribable, to define the indefinable, to speak of the unspeakable, and the only way to do that is to come at it obliquely, to adopt the way of the poet, the way of metaphor and the use of imaginative figures of speech that can make tangible the intangible and enable us to lay hold upon truths that are truer than mere facts, truths having to do with meaning and value rather than process and measurement. Religious truth, like poetic truth, is always the product of an inspired imagination. Whether we are believers or atheists, the God that we honor or the God whose existence we deny is in either case the God we have imagined, or the God that someone before us has imagined and described for us. We have been told that He is our Creator, our Heavenly Father, our Lord, our Rock of Ages, our Shepherd, our Haven in the storm, our Judge, our Savior... the author of the "Battle Hymn of the Republic" has described Him as the wielder of a "terrible swift sword" of justice, the great reformer, Martin Luther,

has defined Him as a "Mighty Fortress," and the writers of
the Presbyterian *Westminster Shorter Catechismn* have called
Him a "spirit, infinite, eternal and unchangeable..."[2] And
all of these powerful images came from the minds and
imaginations of people who lived in a world far different
from the one we know today. Their daily experiences— the
fields from which they harvested the comparative likenesses
that helped them to think about the nature of the eternal and
the meaning of the mystery that surrounds us—were very
different from those of twenty-first century people. Today we
have no intimate knowledge of "terrible swift swords" and
little but a tourist's acquaintance with "mighty fortresses,"
and as citizens of a scientific age, we have trouble grasping
the notion of "infinite unchangeability." J. B. Phillips was
writing in the 1950s when he spoke of the need to enlarge
our concept of God. He might be even more troubled today
to discover how small, indeed, our Western God has become
and how much more remote. The celestial real estate where
our imagined deity has his throne has gotten lost among the
billions and billions of galaxies that make up our enormously
expanding universe.

It is not, however, simply because our names for the deity
are old and out of step with our present knowledge about
the universe and its origins that they need to be traded in
for new ones. The problem with the God we have imagined
is far more serious than merely the worn out and outdated
condition of the words we have employed to describe
him. The problem is that what we believe in, how we give
form and content to what we deem to be ultimately true

about our world and our life in it will go a long way toward determining how we behave in and toward that world, and in that respect, the traditional metaphors that have shaped our belief in God have gotten us into a lot of trouble. In the West, and particularly in the Judeo-Christian-Islamic world, we have consistently imagined a God who has His being separately from our own existence and that of our earthly place of residence; as the architect is separate from the building he designs, as the carpenter and brick mason are separate from its construction, as the landlord is separate from the property he manages and from the tenants to whom he leases living space. And this image of a God who exists apart from His creation, who, as it were, stands over against us as a separate being—even though it has been tempered somewhat by metaphors of a loving father, caring provider, and merciful savior—has nevertheless had a profound, and not very positive, effect on the way we have treated the living space provided for us and how we have behaved toward the other creatures who share with us our natural home. Indeed, it may well be that the dire problems we are now facing as a result of our exploitative and destructive attitude toward our environment are to be traced directly to the hierarchy of values that derive from this man upstairs metaphor that has characterized popular religion in Western culture.

So, why did we humans ever imagine the existence of that separate God person in the first place? In 1993, Karen Armstrong, a former Catholic nun and now a recognized authority on the history of Western religions, published a fascinating book with an intriguing title: *A History of God:*

The 4,000-year Quest of Judaism, Christianity and Islam. In
the opening line of the first chapter, she writes, "In the
beginning, human beings created a God who was the First
Cause of all things and Ruler of heaven and earth."[3] So,
strictly speaking, despite its imposing title, the book is not
so much a "history of God" as it is the history of a very
human idea. It is the story of how our ideas about God
developed within certain Western cultures and how we
have come to imagine specifically the kind of God we have
imagined. In her study, however, Ms. Armstrong only goes
back four thousand years to the time of the Old Testament
patriarch, Abraham. In reality, the notion of a supernatural
being or beings goes back a whole lot further than that. It
goes back, I believe, all the way to the early morning of our
Homo sapien self awareness. If she is correct in her assertion
that human beings created God in that early beginning,
why did we do that? We surely didn't just think it up for no
particular reason. In that beginning time there must surely
have been a question in our minds—more likely a whole
syndrome of questions—to which it dawned on us that a
supernatural creator might just be the answer. So, what was
the question? I believe that if we think really hard about
that, we can "remember" what might have been bothering
us humans even way back then. I think the questions started
coming pretty soon after we exited the Eden of our pre-
human existence. We had a problem, you see. *We had simply
evolved beyond the comfort level of our previous natural animal life.*
Having crossed that evolutionary bridge, we found ourselves
in some very uncomfortable territory. There was something

245

definitely unnatural about us. As a species we were a walking contradiction, and that caused us a lot of anxiety. Our new self-consciousness, which opened to us wondrous worlds of possibilities, also brought with it a heavy load of troubling questions: Who *are* we? Where did we *come* from? What are we *doing* here? What is our proper *place* in the world? Why do we have to *die*? What *happens* to our unique self-identity when we die? Thus were born, in the early dawn of our consciousness of ourselves as a peculiar species, the universal spiritual questions, which have fertilized the fecund seedbed of the religious imagination throughout human history. And the germ of an idea of God began to grow.

Of course, God did not start out His life in our inspired imaginations as a fully developed, separately existing creator-person. In our search for answers to our peculiar situation, we tried out a lot of different sense-making metaphors: the sun, planets, animals, even trees...Over the eons, an enormous, richly populated assembly of gods and goddesses have shown up in the hallways of our religious imagining as possible ways of capturing the truth about our strangely troubled existence. It may have been memories of our animal preexistence, deeply buried in our psyches, that suggested to us at different places and different times the deification of ibises, ravens, falcons, jackals, leopards, bears, etc., but those kinds of metaphors could not have satisfied many of us for very long. The one thing we knew with any certainty about ourselves even back then was that we were different from any other form of life that we saw around us. We were special; that was obvious. And I suspect that by the time we had lived with that awareness for a while, we were so convinced of our uniqueness in comparison to the lower animals—despite our physical similarities—that most of us could no longer have imagined that our existence was in any way directly connected familially to theirs. So, how did we come to conceive of a "First Cause" in the shape of a person, a super powerful male figure? There are perhaps some clues to that in the words we still use today when we describe the deity, words like, lord, master, king, ruler, father. Since all metaphors of comparison for intangible truths are always drawn from the world of our daily experiences, it was probably only after we had separated ourselves into tribal groups with leaders and warriors who fought for us in competition with other groups, that there sparked in us the notion of a God who was a supernatural version of a tribal lord. And "Our Father who art in heaven" came into being.

There is, as well, plenty of paleontological evidence that some of us, very early on, imagined our maker as a female figure, and in many ways the birth mother metaphor would seem a quite natural way to picture the creator who gives us life. Why the goddess ultimately failed generally to capture our religious imaginations we can only speculate. Maybe it was just *too* natural to imagine the origin of our species in terms of that very earthy, natal process that we share with those lower mammalian creatures from whom we were, after all, trying to separate ourselves. Or maybe the demise of the feminine deity was simply the result of the human male's anxious, testosterone-driven need to dominate. But if we were seeking a metaphor that would reinforce the best of our human tendencies, the image of a chest-beating warrior king hardly seems a better choice than that of the gentle mother goddess. Nevertheless, He won out. It took a long time, but ultimately, at least among those of us who populated Europe and the West, the Old Man in the Sky took over our religious imaginations as the sole "ruler of heaven and earth." All other gods and goddesses were vanquished and He became so totally the accepted answer to our spiritual dilemma that we almost forgot what the questions were. And for most of us, that was okay. By then there had arisen in society a whole priestly profession (made up mostly of men) whose only job was to act as interceders between that God-person and His earthly children. There was no need for the average person to bother with the troubling questions. We just had to believe what the established religious authorities told us. Life might not be all that perfect in the small details, but the big picture was pretty much settled. God was in His heaven and all was basically right with the world. Wasn't that what we wanted to believe?

Then, in 1543, when the priestly class had been settled firmly for some time into the saddle of Western society's progress, an obscure Polish cleric named Nicholas Copernicus committed the heresy of believing his eyes instead of what his religious superiors told him to believe. On the basis of what he thought he was seeing in the movements of the planets and the stars, he had the audacity to suggest that the official religious teaching about the earth's place in the universe might not be accurate. What he put on paper about his hypothesis was hardly noticed until a certain Italian named Galileo Galilei, who had also developed the "devilish" habit of believing only what his eyes told him about the world around him, made himself a crude little "spyglass" of a telescope and proceeded to demonstrate by careful observation that what Copernicus had only speculated was indeed a fact: the earth is not the center of the universe, despite what the Genesis story of creation might otherwise imply. The scientific method that had languished under the weight of ecclesiastical dogma following the days of Greece and Rome was given a new impetus, and ever since then, multitudes of men and women, trained in the art of observation and dedicated to the notion that the only facts about our world are those that can be demonstrated to be true by experimentation and testing, have been developing a theoretical model of the universe that does not require the existence of a supernatural power to explain its operation.

It was not, however, until the late nineteenth century that science, in the work of Charles Darwin and his followers, dealt its most devastating blow to the traditional metaphors of Western religious belief. Darwin's discoveries made widely believable for the first time what had previously seemed simply unimaginable. He reconnected us to the natural world. He showed us that we humans arrived on earth not by means of a special creative act, but by direct biological descent from the apes that early roamed the forests and savannas of Africa. He took away the necessity for explaining our origin by imagining a separate supernatural creator. Isn't that what we had wanted to know? How we came to be here? Wasn't it to answer that question that we had invented all of those gods and goddesses in the first place? So, here was the plain truth about our origin as a species. And here was the new answer to the old question in the catechism of my childhood: Question: Who made you? Answer today: No one made me; I evolved from my simian ancestors.

One day, about the time I was beginning to see the end of this literary investigation into the wreckage of my former religious belief, I happened to be listening to our local public radio station, and I heard a promotional announcement for an upcoming call-in discussion program on the subject, "Has science made belief in God obsolete?" I wasn't around when the program aired, so I wasn't able to listen in, and now I am kind of glad for that. The question as posed seemed so directly applicable to my own search that it might have been aimed directly at me, and I felt that I needed to come up with my own answer to it without the distraction of other people's responses, however wise and insightful they might have been. It certainly is a question deserving of a more thorough consideration than is possible in the span of a sixty-minute radio talk show. So, after much thought and careful consideration, *has* science made belief in God obsolete? Yes, in a sense, it certainly has. But I take exception to the way in which the question is phrased. It is far too narrowly framed, and I don't believe that it adequately addresses the real issue at stake in the discussion between science and religion.

When my father asked me all those years ago if I had lost my faith, he was basically asking me whether or not I still believed all the things that I had been taught to believe during my early upbringing in the Church. I could have told him, no, I didn't believe all that stuff any more. I could have told him that when I left the ministry I hadn't just changed jobs, but that I had walked out on that whole religious part of my life. I could have told him that I now lived in an almost totally secular world where any attempt at "God talk" was likely to be an embarrassment and that religion was something you outgrew, sort of like the Christmas fantasy of Santa Claus. But I didn't tell him all of that. I didn't tell him because, on one level, I just didn't want to get into another argument with him. On a deeper level, however, I couldn't tell him that because I didn't want to break his heart. Ultimately, however, I couldn't tell him that because the truth of it was just not that simple. So I mumbled something about just not being comfortable any longer with the old religious language. And, surprisingly, that feeble attempt at a reply to his pained question has turned out to be the real truth of the matter for me. I am sorry that I could not have better explained to him what I meant by that, but back then, I had not yet thought it through for myself. But it really is the crux of the matter, I think. And it is the real issue in the so-called war between science and religion. Science has not made *spirituality and religion* obsolete. Science has merely described a universe in which the metaphors, the figures of speech, that we have traditionally used to express our responses to the mystery surrounding our lives have grown stale and archaic and practically useless as ways of thinking about and sharing our feelings about the meanings of our living and loving and dying. Science has not made religion obsolete any more than it has made poetry and art obsolete. It has not made religion obsolete because it has not made the spiritual questions obsolete. We humans will not stop asking the questions that first occurred to us when we found ourselves out here in this troubling world of ambiguous self-consciousness. Who is this contradictory being we have become? What does the manner of our origin say about the meaning of our lives? Now that we have learned to dream great dreams, how do we learn to live happily with our animal limitations, including our deaths? And how do we live with the disappointments that come when our dream castles all turn out to be bungalows, and when we have to watch our hopes for our children prematurely fade and die, when we have to face our own failures to be the best that we could have been? Why, despite our superior intellect, do we humans keep falling into the same old holes of self-destructive behavior? Why can't we stop hurting each other and fouling the planetary nest that is our only home? As an individual, how shall I overcome the fundamental loneliness that is an inevitable component of my unique individuality? How shall I find and maintain a sense of connectedness in a world populated by billions of individuals just like me, each clamoring for a place of his own? In what sense does my little life matter at all in the big picture of this overcrowded ark adrift in the vast ocean of the universe? In such a world as this, does faith have any future at all?

It is too soon to know what kinds of new answers to the old questions, new figures of speech, new metaphors for the mystery, new poetic images for the sacred, we will imagine to replace the ones that have dominated Western religious thinking for so many centuries. It is too soon to know if we will ever again have the kind of religious consensus that will shape culture in the way the Judeo-Christian tradition has shaped the Western mind. Or if such a consensus is even desirable. It is too soon to know if we will ever again share a story, have a common mythology, by which we define ourselves as individuals and as a society. I have already suggested what might be the broad outlines of such a story, should it occur to us, but it remains to be seen if we will ever again know such a common faith. But because we will never stop asking the basic human questions about our lives, I think we will never stop trying for answers. Nor will we ever stop exercising our religious imaginations, if only tentatively as seeking individuals.

So, as a seeking individual myself, I offer my personal "Confession of Faith." Mind you, I put forward this statement of belief as a tentative suggestion, not as a definitive answer even to my own questions, much less to anyone else's. This is just where I find myself right now:

I believe in *Life*, one self-creating and transcendent *Life*, one dynamic, changing, expanding *Life*, one *Life* in the process of becoming itself, one *Life* that is the origin of all the multiform expressions of itself that exist throughout the universe.

I believe that I and you and every living thing that has, does, or ever will exist—zoological or botanical, animate or inanimate—are "words" in the vocabulary of *Life's* expression of itself.

I believe that planet earth is one location in the universe where conditions have come together to enable *Life* to experiment with a diverse and increasingly complex language of self-expression. There may be other such locations, other planets in other galaxies, where *Life* is trying out dialects different from the natural language of earth, and if there are such places and other forms out there that *Life* has breathed into being, they may be quite different from us, but they will be compatible with us because *Life* is one and the laws of physical existence are consistent throughout the universe.

I believe that the story of the evolution of life on earth is a sacred story. I believe that what Charles Darwin came up with was not simply the best and most convincing scientific theory to explain the process by which life on earth has developed, but beyond that he gave us the basic outline of what may really be "the greatest story ever told." What he and his heirs in the scientific community have brilliantly described for us is the mechanism of natural selection by which life on earth has evolved from primitive, simple stages through constant experimentation, through trial and error, to ever more complex, more sentient forms. To scientists, with their determination to attend only to what is measurable and demonstrable in the laboratory, that may appear to be a purely genetically automated process, but when eyed from the slant of the spiritual/religious imagination, that cooly rational explanation of how things came to be can become a different story altogether. I believe that what I am hearing when I read the story of evolution is the story of *Life* in search of form, *Life* in search of shapes in which to cast itself, *Life* in search of a language by which to express itself.

I believe that humans represent only the latest stage in the evolution *on earth* of *Life's* language of being, but that we are still evolving and will continue to do so as long as earth remains a life-supporting habitat. Nevertheless, I believe that humans have already reached a level of development that distinguishes us as unique in comparison to all of our animal kin. And I believe that our uniqueness lies in the level of self-consciousness that we have achieved, which enables us to step outside ourselves, as it were, and to contemplate our lives and our world with an objectivity unavailable to any other earthly species. I believe that, in us, *Life* itself has achieved self-consciousness. That makes us, in a sense, the medium of *Life's* conversation with itself. In us, *Life* has become personal.

I believe that the most important human quality to result from our evolving self-consciousness is our capacity to love. I believe, further, that the evolutionary antecedents of the compassionate caring we have learned to feel and to express toward our fellow beings can be seen in the behavior of other, less highly evolved species, in their genetically programmed patterns of communal cooperation, of mating, reproducing and caring for their offspring. And this suggests to me that the story of evolution might itself be read as a testimony to the direction in which *Life* has been developing all along. Thus do I dare to believe that love is the meaning that lies beneath the mystery of *Life's* constant and continuing incarnation of itself in the myriads of living forms that grace ours and, perhaps, other planets. I believe that nature, as we know it on earth, is *Life's* love song to itself. Love is the purpose for which we have evolved into *Homo sapiens*. Love is the definition of *Life*. *Life* is Love. Love is *Life*.

I believe, however, that we humans are yet a contradictory and troubled species. And I believe furthermore that most of our discontent and our self-destructive and community-disruptive behaviors stem from our failure to find a comfortable compromise between the animal and spiritual halves of our natures, to live serenely with our contradictions. Perhaps, in time, we will simply evolve into creatures to whom such a balanced acceptance of ourselves comes naturally, and by whom our animal limitations, including the finality of our deaths, will be embraced as natural a part of our lives as our capacity to dream dreams and to be ever reaching for their fulfillment. In the meantime, I believe that it is possible for us to choose the wisdom of self-acceptance over the follies of denial and pretension. We can either fight against the facts of our lives and our deaths, or we can makes friends with them. We can go on anxiously pretending to the exemptions of heaven, or we can relax and accept our mortality—as well as our special capabilities—as merely the highest evolved of our cousins in the animal family of *Life's* expression of itself. It seems to me that it was something like this that Jesus had in mind when he counseled his followers to let go of their lives in order to find them.

Life calls to life. *Life* loves itself in all the living forms in which it shapes itself. *Life* calls to you and me to love ourselves as we are loved, and in turn to love all other living forms, which, after all, are, like us, the "words" of *Life's* self expression.

(Author's note: Readers might find it interesting and useful to read again the last few paragraphs, substitutng for my word, Life, *whatever words seem personally meaningful as a part of their own re-imagining of whatever energy, power, force, being, essence, mind, spirit, truth, transcendence...lies at the heart of the mystery of ours and the universe's existence.)*

References

Words, Words, Words:

[1]*The Taming of the Shrew*, William Shakespeare, Mineola, New York,
   Dover Publications, 1997.

[2]*The American College Dictionary*, C. L. Barnhart, Editor, New York,
   Random House, 1962.

[3]*Complete Poems*, Carl Sandburg, New York, Harcourt,
   Brace & World, Inc., 1950. "Fog", P. 33.

[4]*Hunting Season*, Nevada Barr, New York, G. P. Putnam's Sons, 2002, p.172.

[5]The *Nashville Tennessean*, Nashville, August 1, 2009, p.1.

Headbanging on Sacred Walls:

[1]"Theological Declaration of Barmen," written by Karl Barth,
   signed by representatives of the German Confessional Churches,
   May, 1934. Available online.

[2]*The Cost of Discipleship*, Dietrich Bonhoeffer, New York,
   Macmillan, 1966.

[3]*The Deep South Says Never*, John Bartlow Martin, New York,
   Ballantine Books, 1957. "Black Belt Town," pp.43 - 77.

[4]The history of Summerton, South Carolina's struggle to maintain
   segregated schools is available online. Google "Summerton, South
   Carolina, school desegregation."

257

[5]*Beyond Belief*, Elaine Pagels, New York, Random House, 2003.
[6]*The Age of Anxiety*, W. H. Auden, New York, Random House,1947. p.42

Truth Is Where You Find It:
[1]*Porgy and Bess*, Opera, 1935, music by George Gershwin, lyrics by
   Ira Gershwin, based on the novel and play, *Porgy*, by DuBose and
   Dorothy Heyward.
[2]*English Romantic Poetry and Prose*, Russell Noyes, New York, Oxford
   University Press, 1956. "My Heart Leaps Up," William
   Wordsworth, p. 309.
[3]*The Little Prince*, Antoine de Saint-Exupery, New York, Harcourt,
   Brace Jovanovich, Inc.,1943
[4]Noyes, p.317.
[5]*The Power of Myth*, Joseph Campbell with Bill Moyers, New York,
   Doubleday & Co., 1988.

Well I'll Be a Monkey's…:
[1]*Audubon Bird Guide, Eastern Land Birds*, Richard Pough, New York,
   Doubleday & Co., 1946.
[2]*Alabama Birds*, Thomas A. Imhof, Tuscaloosa, University of Alabama

   Press, 1962.
[3]*Summer For the Gods, the Scopes Trial ands America's Continuing Debate Over
   Science and Religion*, Edward J. Larson, Newark, Basic Books, 1997.
[5]"Was Darwin Wrong?" David Quammen, *The National Geographic*,
   Vol. 206, No. 5, November, 2004, pp. 3–31.
[6]*Becoming Human, Evolution and Human Uniqueness*, Ian Tattersall, New
   York, Harcourt, Brace& Company, 1998. p 216.
[7]Tattersall, p. 217 - 218.

[8]Tattersall, p. 219.

[9]*Our Birds in Their Haunts*, Hibbert J. Langille, Boston, S. E. Cassino & Company, 1884, p. 205.

[10]*DuBose Genealogy*, Dorothy Kelly McDowell, Aiken, South Carolina, 1972.

The Devil in the Mirror:

[1]*The Unsilent South, Prophetic Preaching in Racial Crisis*, Donald W. Shriver Jr., Editor, Richmond, John Knox Press, 1965. "My Hometown," Lucius B. DuBose, pp. 84-90.

[2]*When Bad Things Happen to Good People*, Harold Kushner, New York, Anchor Books, 1981.

[3]*Humanity, A Moral History of the Twentieth Century*, Jonathan Glover, New Haven, Yale University Press, 1999. p. 7.

[4]*Care of the Soul*, Thomas More, New York, HarperCollins Publishers, 1992, p. 20.

[5]*Pogo*, Walt Kelly, New York, Simon and Schuster, 1952.

[6]*Atonement*, Ian McEwen, New York, Random House, Inc., 2001, p. 150.

[7]*The Fire Next Time*, James Baldwin, New York, Dell Publishing Company, 1963. "My Dungeon Shook: Letter to My Nephew on the One Hundredth Anniversary of the Emancipation," pp. 11–22.

[8]*Lies My Teachers Told Me*, James W. Loewen, New York, Touchstone Books, Simon and Schuster, 1996. p. 143.

Tell Me a New Story:

[1]*Skeptics and True Believers*, Chet Raymo, New York, Walker and Company, 1999, p. 2.

[2]*Eat, Pray, Love*, Elizabeth Gilbert, New York, Penguin Books, 2007, p. 207.

[3]*Living With Darwin, Evolution, Design, and the Future of Faith*, Philip
   Kitcher, New York, Oxford University Press, 2007, p 15.

[4]*Life, A Natural History of the First Four Billion Years of Life on Earth*,
   Richard Fortey, New York, Random House, 1997, p. 304.

[5]Raymo, p. 260.

[6]*A History of the English Speaking Peoples: Volume I, The Birth of Britain*,
   Winston Churchill, New York, Dodd, Mead & Company, 1956, p. 45.

[7]Raymo, p. 260.

No Magic Kingdom:

[1]*Frontline*, Public Broadcasting System, WGBH, Boston,*Faith and Doubt
   at Ground Zero*, aired originally on September 2, 2002.

[2]*Questions For Ecclesiastes*, poems by Mark Jarman, Brownsville,
   Oregon, Story Line Press, 1997; "Unholy Sonnets No. Six," p. 56.

[3]*Teaching a Stone to Talk*, Annie Dillard, New York, Harper & Row,
   1982, p. 68.

Conclusion: The God We Have Imagined:

[1]*Your God is Too Small*, J. B. Phillips, New York, The Macmillan
   Company, 1956.

[2]*The Westminster Shorter Catechism*, The General Assembly of the
   Presbyterian Church in the United States, Richmond, The Board
   of Christian Education, 1965.

[3]*A History of God: the 4,000-Year Quest of Judaism, Christianity and Islam*,
   Karen Armstrong, New York, Alfred A. Knopf, 1993, p. 3.

ACKNOWLEDGEMENTS

AN IMPORTANT TRUTH I have had to learn over the years is that almost nothing I have ever accomplished was solely my own doing. There are so many people, family members, friends, colleagues, teachers, mentors, who must share the credit for anything worthwhile that I have done. And the sad thing about waiting so late in life to publish my first book is that so many who contributed so much to this project, if only indirectly, are no longer alive to receive my gratitude. To those who contributed directly to its fruition I owe many thanks, among them four special longtime friends and colleagues, each of whom read the entire manuscript, sometimes in several installments and always unedited, and who were gracious in their criticism and encouragement: Bill Dantzler, Robert Hull, Pat McGeachy, and Barry Buxkamper. Thanks are due my brother, Cantey, who offered a unique perspective with regard to both the autobiographical and ecclesiastical parts of the story. A retired Presbyterian minister himself, and also a late blooming artist, now in his eighties, he is still reading and thinking and questioning. I also express my appreciation to three others who read parts of the manuscript as a work in progress and offered constructive criticism: John Burkey, Dr. William Dutton, and Bill Willis.

Special thanks are due to John Egerton for his advice, his hard questions, his reality checks, and for shepherding me across the rocky fields of modern day publishing, and to my publisher, Peter Honsberger of Cold River Studio, for turning my solitary re-imaginings into a beautifully designed book to be shared with others. I owe an immeasurable debt of gratitude to my editor, Rachel Fichter, whose literary expertise and incisive corrections and suggestions have made the final product far more readable than my original manuscript. And finally a huge thank-you to Lenda, my wife, best friend, partner, and devil's advocate throughout this process, who only occasionally lost patience with her analog husband's bewilderment at the technical mysteries of the digital world.

CPSIA information can be obtained at www.ICGtesting.com
Printed in the USA
BVOW012147230112

281220BV00001B/7/P